D

Mike Brett

Series Editor: Marian Cox

…n or b…

Much Ado About Nothing

William Shakespeare

Philip Allan Updates
Market Place
Deddington
Oxfordshire
OX15 0SE
tel: 01869 338652
www.philipallan.co.uk

© Philip Allan Updates 2006

ISBN-13 978-1-84489-411-6
ISBN-10 1-84889-411-8

Printed by Raithby, Lawrence & Co Ltd, Leicester

Environmental information
The paper on which this title is printed is sourced from mills using wood from
managed, sustainable forests.

P00683

Contents

Introduction

Aims of the guide

The purpose of this Student Text Guide to *Much Ado About Nothing* is to enable you to organise your thoughts and responses to the play, to deepen your understanding of key features and aspects, and to help you to address the particular requirements of examination questions in order to obtain the best possible grade. It will also prove useful to those of you writing a coursework piece on the play by providing summaries, lists, analyses and references to help with the content and construction of the assignment. Line references in this guide refer to the *New Penguin Shakespeare* edition of the play.

The Text Guidance section consists of a series of subsections that examine key aspects of the play, including contexts, interpretations and controversies. Emboldened terms within the Text Guidance section are glossed in 'Literary terms and concepts' on pp. 67–70.

The final section, Questions and Answers, includes mark schemes, exemplar essay plans and samples of marked work.

Assessment Objectives

The Assessment Objectives (AOs) for A-level English Literature are common to all boards:

AO1	communicate clearly the knowledge, understanding and insight appropriate to literary study, using appropriate terminology and accurate and coherent written expression
AO2i	respond with knowledge and understanding to literary texts of different types and periods
AO2ii	respond with knowledge and understanding to literary texts of different types and periods, exploring and commenting on relationships and comparisons between literary texts
AO3	show detailed understanding of the ways in which writers' choices of form, structure and language shape meanings
AO4	articulate independent opinions and judgements, informed by different interpretations of literary texts by other readers
AO5i	show understanding of the contexts in which literary texts are written and understood

| AO5ii | evaluate the significance of cultural, historical and other contextual influences on literary texts and study |

A summary and paraphrase of each Assessment Objective is given below and would be worth memorising:

AO1	clarity of written communication
AO2	informed personal response in relation to time and genre (literary context)
AO3	the creative literary process (context of writing)
AO4	critical and interpretative response (context of reading)
AO5	evaluation of influences (cultural context)

Much Ado About Nothing has a total weighting of 20–30%, divided as follows:

| Edexcel | AO2ii – 10%; AO4 – 5%; AO5ii – 5% Total – 20% |
| AQA Spec A | AO1 – 8%; AO2i – 10%; AO3 – 7%; AO4 – 5% Total – 30% |

Note the different weighting of Assessment Objectives between the different examining boards for the same text. It is essential that you pay close attention to the AOs, and their weighting, for the board for which you are entered. These are what the examiner will be looking for, and you must address them *directly* and *specifically*, in addition to proving general familiarity with and understanding of the text, and being able to present an argument clearly, relevantly and convincingly.

Remember, the examiners are seeking above all else evidence of an *informed personal response* to the text. A revision guide such as this can help you to understand the text and to form your own opinions, and can suggest areas to think about, but it cannot replace your own ideas and responses as an individual reader.

Revision advice

For the examined units it is possible that either brief or more extensive revision will be necessary because the original study of the text took place some time previously. It is therefore as well to know how to go about revising and which tried and tested methods are considered the most successful for literature exams at all levels, from GCSE to degree finals.

There are no short cuts to effective exam revision; the only one way to know a text well, and to know your way around it in an exam, is to have done the necessary studying. If you use the following six-stage method for both open- and closed-book revision, you will not only revisit and reassess all your previous work on the text in a manageable way but will be able to distil, organise and retain your knowledge.

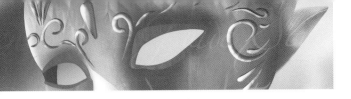

(1) Between a month and a fortnight before the exam, depending on your schedule (a simple list of stages with dates to display in your room, not a work of art!), you will need to reread the text, this time taking stock of all the underlinings and marginal annotations as well. As you read, collect onto sheets of A4 the essential ideas and quotations as you come across them. The acts of selecting key material and recording it as notes are natural ways of stimulating thought and aiding memory.

(2) Reread the highlighted areas and marginal annotations in your critical extracts and background handouts, and add anything useful from them to your list of notes and quotations. Then reread your previous essays and the teacher's comments. As you look back through essays written earlier in the course, you should have the pleasant sensation of realising that you could now write much better on the text than you could then. You will also discover that much of your huge file of notes is redundant or repeated, and that you have changed your mind about some beliefs, so that the distillation process is not too daunting. Selecting what is important is the way to crystallise your knowledge and understanding.

(3) During the run-up to the exam you need to do lots of practice essay plans to help you identify any gaps in your knowledge and give you practice in planning in 5–8 minutes. Past paper titles for you to plan are provided in this guide, some of which can be done as full timed essays — and marked strictly according to exam criteria — which will show whether length and timing are problematic for you. If you have not seen a copy of a real exam paper before you take your first module, ask to see a past paper so that you are familiar with the layout, rubric and types of question. For each text you are studying for the examination you need to know exactly which Assessment Objectives are being tested and where the heaviest weighting falls, as well as whether it is a closed- or open-book exam. It would also be helpful if your teacher shared with you the examiners' reports on past papers.

(4) About a week before the exam, reduce your two or three sides of A4 notes to a double-sided postcard of very small, dense writing. Collect a group of key words by once again selecting and condensing, and use abbreviations for quotations (first and last word), and character and place names (initials). Choosing and writing out the short quotations will help you to focus on the essential issues, and to recall them quickly in the exam. Make sure that your selection covers the main themes and includes examples of imagery, language, style, comments on character, examples of irony and other significant aspects of the text. Previous class discussion and essay writing will have indicated which quotations are useful for almost any title; pick those that can serve more than one purpose. In this way a minimum number of quotations can have maximum application.

(**5**) You now have in a compact, accessible form all the material for any possible essay title. There are only half a dozen themes relevant to a literary text so if you have covered these, you should not meet with any nasty surprises when you read the exam questions. You don't need to refer to your file of paperwork again, or even to the text. For the few days before the exam, you can read through your handy postcard whenever and wherever you get the opportunity. Each time you read it, which will only take a few minutes, you are reminding yourself of all the information you will be able to recall in the exam to adapt to the general title or to support an analysis of particular passages.

(**6**) A fresh, active mind works wonders, and information needs time to settle, so don't try to cram just before the exam. Get a good night's sleep the night before. Then you will be able to enter the exam room with all the confidence of a well-prepared candidate.

Coursework

It is possible that you are doing *Much Ado About Nothing* as a Shakespeare or other coursework text. If so, you must be sure that your title, negotiated with your teacher, fits the Assessment Objectives and their respective weighting for your board. Coursework for all boards must be between 1,500 and 2,000. If you are obliged, or choose, to write two pieces (depending on the board), consideration will need to be given to how the two relate to each other and cover different aspects of the text without overlap. The coursework writing process differs from an examination in being more leisurely and more supported by the discussion and drafting stages, but the issues of the text remain the same, as does the need for a relevant, focused response to the title.

Coursework should be word-processed in the interests of presentation, consideration for the examiner, and ease of alteration for the student. There are a number of key stages in the coursework writing process:

- Once your title is decided and you are familiar with the Assessment Objectives, reread the play and all the notes and annotations you have made, extracting what is relevant for your title.
- With teacher guidance, read some background material and critical essays, and collect relevant information from them. Keep a list of books and articles consulted. Rephrase any ideas you borrow from elsewhere.
- Write a one-page essay plan, consisting of subheadings and main points, and show it to your teacher to ensure you have covered the title fully and have adopted an appropriate essay structure.
- Write a draft of the essay, roughly the right length, based on your plan. Use details, examples and quotations from the text to support your points.

- Read through your draft, making sure that you have remained focused on the question and answered it fully. Submit your draft to your teacher in good time.
- When your draft is returned, put into practice the comments offered to help you improve your essay and its grade, and adjust the length if necessary.
- Produce the final version, improving content, expression and accuracy where possible. Check the final word count. Include a bibliography listing the texts you have quoted from or consulted.
- After a final read through, putting yourself in the position of the reader, make last-minute adjustments and submit your essay — before the deadline.

Writing examination essays

Essay content

One of the key skills you are being asked to demonstrate at A-level is the ability to select and tailor your knowledge of the text and its background to the question set in the exam paper. In order to reach the highest levels, you need to avoid 'pre-packaged' essays that lack focus, relevance and coherence, and that simply contain everything you know about the text. Be ruthless in rejecting irrelevant material, after considering whether it can be made relevant by a change of emphasis. Aim to cover the whole question, not just part of it; your response needs to demonstrate breadth and depth, covering the full range of text elements: character, event, theme and language. Only half a dozen essay approaches are possible for any set text, though they may be phrased in a variety of ways, and they are likely to refer to the key themes of the text. Preparation of the text therefore involves extensive discussion and practice at manipulating these core themes so that there should be no surprises in the exam. An apparently new angle is more likely to be something familiar presented in an unfamiliar way, and you should not panic or reject the choice of question because you think you know nothing about it.

Exam titles are open-ended in the sense that there is no obvious right answer, and you would therefore be unwise to give a dismissive, extreme or entirely one-sided response; the question would not have been set if the answer were not debatable. An ability and willingness to see both sides is an Assessment Objective and shows independence of judgement as a reader. Don't be afraid to explore the issues and don't try to tie the text into one neat interpretation. If there is ambiguity it is likely to be deliberate on the part of the author and must be discussed; literary texts are complex and often paradoxical, and it would be a misreading of them to suggest that there is only one possible interpretation. You are not expected, however, to argue equally strongly or extensively for both sides of an argument, since personal opinion is an important factor. It is advisable to deal with the alternative view at the beginning of your response, and then construct your own view as the main part of the essay. This makes it less likely that you will appear to cancel out your own line of argument.

Choosing the right question

The first skill you must show when presented with the exam paper is the ability to choose the better, for you, of the two questions on your text where there is a choice. This is not to say that you should always go for the same type of essay (whole-text or passage-based), and if there is one question you don't feel happy with for any reason, you should seriously consider the other, even if it is not the type you normally prefer. It is unlikely but possible that a question contains a word you are not sure you know the meaning of, in which case it would be safer to choose the other one.

Don't be tempted to choose a question because of its similarity to one you have already done. Freshness and thinking on the spot usually produce a better answer than attempted recall of a previous essay that may have received only a mediocre mark in the first place. The exam question is unlikely to have exactly the same focus and your response may seem 'off centre' as a result, as well as stale and perfunctory in expression.

Essay questions fall into the following categories: close section analysis and relation to whole text; characterisation; setting and atmosphere; structure and effectiveness; genre; language and style; themes and issues. Remember, however, that themes are relevant to all essays, and that analysis, not just description, is always required.

Once you have decided which exam question to attempt, follow the procedure below for whole-text and passage-based, open- and closed-book essays.

(1) Underline all the key words in the question and note how many parts the question has.

(2) Plan your answer, using aspects of the key words and parts of the question as subheadings, in addition to themes. Aim for 10–12 ideas. Check that the Assessment Objectives are covered.

(3) Support your argument by selecting the best examples of characters, events, imagery and quotations to prove your points. Remove ideas for which you can find no evidence.

(4) Structure your answer by grouping and numbering your points in a logical progression. Identify the best general point to keep for the conclusion.

(5) Introduce your essay with a short paragraph setting the context and defining the key words in the question as broadly, but relevantly, as possible.

(6) Write the rest of the essay, following your structured plan but adding extra material if it occurs to you. Paragraph your writing and consider expression, especially sentence structure and vocabulary choices, as you write. Signal changes in the direction of your argument with paragraph openers such as 'Furthermore' and 'However'. Include plenty of short, integrated quotations and use the words of the text rather than your own where possible. Employ technical terms appropriately, and write concisely and precisely, avoiding vagueness and ambiguity.

(7) Your conclusion should sound conclusive and make it clear that you have answered the question. It should be an overview of the question and the text, not a repetition or a summary of points already made.

(8) Cross out your plan with a neat diagonal line.

(9) Check your essay for content, style, clarity and accuracy. With neat crossings-out, correct errors of fact, spelling, grammar and punctuation. Improve expression if possible, and remove any repetition and irrelevance. Add clarification and missing evidence, if necessary, using omission marks or asterisks. Even at this stage good material can be added.

There is no such thing as a perfect or model essay; flawed essays can gain full marks. There is always something more that could have been said, and examiners realise that students have limitations when writing under pressure in timed conditions. You are not penalised for what you didn't say in comparison to some idealised concept of the perfect answer, but are rewarded for the knowledge and understanding you have shown. It is not as difficult as you may think to do well, provided that you know the text in detail and have sufficient essay-writing experience. Follow the process of **choose**, **underline**, **select**, **support**, **structure**, **write** and **check**, and you can't go far wrong.

Text Guidance

LITERATURE

Contexts

The England of the late 1500s, in which Shakespeare wrote *Much Ado About Nothing*, was a period of great scientific and social change. English explorers were involved in ambitious ventures of discovery and colonial expansion, while the Church of England continued to establish itself at home and abroad after Elizabeth took the throne in 1558. The economy was booming, and the population of London was growing at an extraordinary rate.

The traditional Elizabethan world view, which was initially inherited from the Middle Ages, began to break down during this period, and this conflict between new and old ways of thinking is dramatised in the plays of Shakespeare and his contemporaries.

Cultural context

Below are some of the contemporary religious beliefs and social attitudes which throw light on the hopes, fears, thoughts and actions of the characters in *Much Ado About Nothing*.

Chain of being

The Elizabethans inherited from medieval theology the concept of a hierarchical chain of being in which every creature appeared in its ordained position on a ladder descending from God. At the top of the scale was the angel, followed by king, man and woman (in that order) through to animal, vegetable and, finally, mineral. This belief in a divine order was often used to explain the innate inferiority of women to men, thereby maintaining the status quo in the **patriarchal** societies of Elizabethan and Jacobean England. The imbalance between the sexes supplied a fertile source of humour for the majority of Shakespeare's comedies, and even the comic scenes in some of his darker plays. The preponderance of animal imagery in *Much Ado About Nothing* serves to highlight the Elizabethan view that love was a force capable of causing man to abandon his reason in favour of animal instinct, thereby lowering himself to a bestial level.

There are several instances in *Much Ado About Nothing* where Shakespeare seems to call into question the validity of the chain of being. We are not always invited to equate the 'masculine' traits of military prowess and sexual banter with innate superiority, as we see in several grave examples of ill-judgement, by Claudio in particular. Perhaps most significantly, Benedick abandons the bravura of his male companions in favour of Beatrice's compassion and loyalty to Hero, by challenging the man who defames Hero to a duel. Another example of Shakespeare questioning society's conventions and hierarchies is the fact that, in the world of the play, moral sensibility is not, as was widely thought at the time, purely a product of social class. Don John's villainy transcends social borders as he employs Borachio to achieve his evil ends, and a happy ending is only brought about by the intervention of the absurd constable Dogberry and his watchmen.

Nature

The ubiquitous presence of the word 'nature' in Elizabethan literature, and of imagery deriving from it, stems from the contemporary debate about the definition of nature, which has two contradictory aspects: the benevolent and harmonious in contrast to the wild and violent. Most importantly in *Much Ado About Nothing*, the concept of nature is directly linked to familial ties, loyalty and trust. In this respect, the 'unnatural' birth of the bastard Don John is the source of his malignance, just as Edmund's betrayal of his legitimate half-brother in *King Lear* is portrayed by Shakespeare as a fulfilment of his innate bastardy.

Appearance and reality

External appearance was believed by many in Shakespeare's time to be an indicator of what lay within (i.e. goodness or evil). Beauty and whiteness were associated with what was fair, while ugliness and blackness were said to denote vice. Most dangerous of all were those people who were able to conceal their inner evil with an outward display of goodness — a crime of which Claudio accuses Hero in Act IV scene 1. He berates her for her 'Seeming' chastity (54), implying that this makes her 'infidelity' an even worse crime. Hero responds to his accusations of fornication by blushing; an action that produces a mixed response in the onlookers. While Hero's defenders believe this external sign indicates her innocence, Leonato argues that it signifies her guilt.

Reason

The failure of reason was considered to be the cause of the Fall of Man (Adam allowed his love for Eve to overrule his better judgement and obedience to God), and Elizabethans therefore believed it was dangerous to let reason be dominated by passion or any other impulse. Characters in Shakespeare who become uncontrollably emotional are heading for a fall, as their intellect is what distinguishes them from the beasts and allows their actions to be governed by good sense. Claudio's readiness to believe the flimsy evidence of Hero's infidelity therefore constitutes the lowest point in the play for him.

Courtly love

Romance in Shakespeare's time was reflected in the **genre** of **courtly love**, which brought together the masculine ideals of the soldier and the lover, as in the Arthurian legends. By definition the courtly lover had to be a member of high

society and concerned above all with the notions of honour and reputation. Courtly love is represented in *Much Ado About Nothing* by the romance between the handsome soldier-prince Claudio and the governor of Messina's modest daughter, Hero — a love that is jeopardised when Hero's feminine honour is besmirched. The relationship at first develops quickly, and the match is confirmed at a masked ball, fulfilling the courtly requirement of the male knight pursuing his lover (albeit with Don Pedro's help). Unlike most characters in the play, Claudio and Hero both speak largely in **verse**, thus channelling their feelings for one another into chivalrous manners and poetic language. The female object of affection in courtly **romance** was also expected to have rival suitors competing for her hand. This is reflected in Claudio's mistaken assumption that Don Pedro has wooed Hero for himself in Act II scene 1, and once again in his ready belief that his betrothed has betrayed him with another man prior to their wedding.

Women

Students might wonder at the insistence on female chastity in so many Shakespeare plays. The security of society and peace of mind of men was dependent upon women's virginity before marriage (it was a bargaining point in making advantageous matches that would benefit the father's social status) and chastity after marriage (i.e. fidelity). In a society that passed inheritance down the male line, men needed to be sure that their son was really their own and not someone else's bastard, and a man's reputation would be destroyed by an unfaithful wife. Virginity was therefore regarded as the ideal state for women, and also as a test of the nobility of males, since only the higher orders were thought to be able to resist the temptations of the flesh. Virginity and chastity were linked to religion via the Virgin Mary, and damnation was said to await women who had sex out of wedlock. Leonato's reaction to the accusations against Hero in Act IV illustrates the seriousness of the charge, as he asserts that he would prefer her to die than bring shame on herself and her family.

The idea of the fickle female was a classical literary stereotype fostered by the medieval church, the **misogyny** of which was founded on the premise that Eve betrayed her husband and all mankind when she allowed herself to be seduced by an eloquent serpent. Fickle fortune was represented by a woman with a wheel, which she turned at random and without mercy. Don John plays upon this stereotype when attempting to convince Claudio that Hero has been unfaithful to him, calling her 'Leonato's Hero, your Hero, every man's Hero' (III.2.95–96).

As far as the legal status of women is concerned, they were possessions, financially dependent on their fathers, to whom they owed obedience and domestic labour, until they were handed over to the rule of their husbands, whom they had to love, honour and obey, and to whom they were obliged to grant conjugal rights. The consequences of not performing these daughterly and wifely duties were

serious: disobedient women might be disowned and deprived of a home, financial support and a place in society. Having lost both her parents, Beatrice is placed in the care of another male relative (Leonato), who assumes the same parental prerogative over her as he has over Hero. Leonato is therefore the man to whom suitors of either woman must apply for permission to marry, and his honour is intrinsically bound to that of his female charges. Women could only rise through their association with men and their rank, as Margaret illustrates in Act V scene 2, when she cheekily exclaims to Benedick, 'To have no man come over me! Why, shall I always keep below stairs?' (9–10).

Jealousy

Later in his career, Shakespeare explored the theme of jealousy in *Othello* (1604) and *The Winter's Tale* (1610), though its tragic potential is also hinted at in *Much Ado About Nothing*. Because it is irrational, jealousy was viewed as a sudden infection that could not be prevented or cured. It eroded trust and dissolved the bonds holding together marriages, families and the social framework; it created openings for the evil and chaos so greatly feared by Shakespeare's audiences.

A man whose wife betrayed him sexually without his knowledge was known in Elizabethan times as a cuckold. Cuckoldry is a recurrent theme in Shakespeare's plays, and informs a large number of both his comic and tragic plots. A cuckold was said to grow horns on his head as a symbol of his ignorance of his wife's behaviour, and was seen as an object of ridicule. He was perceived as having married a woman with an unnatural sexual appetite, whom he was unable to control. Cuckoldry also has implications for the wider issues of primogeniture and succession; illegitimate children (like Don John) could not be assimilated comfortably into the family structure, and were seen as a threat to the social fabric.

Telling lies

Lying was considered a much more serious offence in Shakespeare's time than it is nowadays. It was a diabolical trick because Satan told Eve lies in the Garden of Eden, causing her to sin. Telling the truth was the way to shame the devil, and lying meant putting one's immortal soul at risk, especially since promises and oaths were thought to be witnessed by heaven. A gentleman's word was assumed to be the truth unless there was a good reason to think otherwise, and it was a grave insult to call someone a liar. Leonato reflects this attitude in Act IV scene 1, as he struggles to believe that anyone of noble birth would lie (150).

Dancing

In Elizabethan courtly society, dancing was an important social skill, which played a crucial role in the forming of romantic relationships. Hosting a lavish dance was also considered a way of displaying social status and wealth, something with which

Leonato is clearly preoccupied during the visit from the important dignitaries Don Pedro and his followers. The masked ball scene in Act II scene 1 of *Much Ado About Nothing* exemplifies how love flourished in these situations, particularly when dancers were liberated by their disguises to be more forthright in expressing their feelings (as we see in *Romeo and Juliet*). Beatrice's bantering with Hero in the same scene illustrates the symbolic value of the dance, as she compares 'wooing, wedding, and repenting' (64–65) to a 'Scotch jig, a measure, and a cinquepace' (65–66).

Duels

In Shakespeare's time, duels were fought between noblemen as a way of settling serious disputes. In this sense, they represent the point at which verbal expression of one's grievances crosses the line into physical violence. Because they took place between the noble classes, duels had specific rules to ensure that combat was fair; in *Hamlet* Osric takes the role of referee in the fight between Laertes and Hamlet, and in *Romeo and Juliet* Mercutio dies because Romeo unexpectedly tries to intervene in his friend's dispute with Tybalt.

Theatrical context

Shakespeare and contemporary theatre

The theatre enjoyed huge popularity in London in the latter part of the sixteenth century. Following the building of the first permanent theatre in London in 1576, another half dozen had been built by the end of Queen Elizabeth's reign in 1603. Shakespeare was particularly associated with the Swan Theatre, and then with the Globe Theatre in Southwark, built in 1599, of which he was a shareholder. During the 1580s a number of professional companies of actors were established, each bearing the name of its patron — for example, the Lord Chamberlain's Men, of which Shakespeare was a member, and the Queen's Men.

During this period many outstandingly talented playwrights and poets were active, including Christopher Marlowe, Edmund Spenser and Sir Philip Sidney. Perhaps because there was a female monarch, there was a flowering of **courtly love** poetry, as exemplified by Beatrice and Benedick's sonnets, and several major sonnet cycles were written. This was known as the Golden Age owing to the flourishing of the arts and the prosperity and comparative peacefulness of the period.

Play-going appealed to all sections of the population; the poor stood as 'groundlings' below the raised stage while the wealthier sat in galleries or boxes. King James, a supporter of Shakespeare's company, the King's Men, was a keen theatre-goer with a personal interest in witchcraft, religion and the role of the monarch. Contemporary playwrights catered for these tastes in their choice of subject matter and creation of characters.

The comedies

Comedy as a **genre** derives from the Greek word *komoidia*, meaning 'village song', although its meaning has evolved over centuries of use. In the Middle Ages and **Renaissance**, the word was used to describe any play which ended happily, and, unlike our conception of comedy today, its most important elements were reconciliation, restoration of order and positive resolution, rather than the power to draw laughs.

In Aristotle's definition of comedy in his *Poetics*, he argued that comedy featured 'ridiculous' characters, who would deter audiences from acting in similarly absurd ways, thus serving the important purpose of giving moral instruction. A contemporary of Shakespeare, Ben Jonson, rehearsed similar arguments in the face of **Puritan** attacks on the theatre in the sixteenth and seventeenth centuries.

When the Folio edition of Shakespeare's works was first published, in 1623, the plays in it were divided under the headings of 'Comedies', 'Tragedies' and 'Histories'. According to this division, there were fourteen comedies, of which *Much Ado About Nothing* was one. The play is usually considered to be of a piece with the other comedies Shakespeare wrote at the end of the sixteenth century, including *Midsummer Night's Dream* (1595), *The Merry Wives of Windsor* (1598), *As You Like It* (1599) and *Twelfth Night* (1599). It is easily distinguished from the darker, morally **ambiguous** 'comedies' he produced later in his career, like *Measure for Measure* (1604), and *All's Well That Ends Well* (1605). Although some critics have suggested that the darker elements of *Much Ado About Nothing* make it problematic, it is still usually categorised as one of Shakespeare's more conventional comic works.

Shakespeare's comedies usually explore the themes of love and marriage, in an idealised 'green', or semi-rural setting, away from the more sinister influences of the city. Common characteristics of the plays include instances of mistaken identity and disguise, frustrated (and finally requited) love, resourceful servants and, of course, lavish weddings. Although audiences tend to know that these plays will end in marriage, tension is built up by the various obstacles that are put in the way of the protagonists. Claudio and Hero, for example, are two young lovers whose marriage is almost prevented by Don John's interference. In this sense the comedies share many of the **motifs** of tragedy, but without the irreversible and disastrous consequences. In *Othello* (1604), Iago seeks to destroy the trust between a couple (Desdemona and Othello) in much the same way as Don John does in *Much Ado About Nothing*, but Iago's plot is horrifically successful. A similar comparison can be made with *Romeo and Juliet* (1595), where the young lovers meet at a masked ball, like Hero and Claudio, but their relationship ends in tragedy because of their parents' actions. Leonato's desire in Act IV scene 1 of *Much Ado About Nothing* to kill Hero for (as he thinks)

shaming his family is not unlike Capulet's outrage at Juliet's refusal to marry Paris in Act III scene 5 of that play:

An you be mine, I'll give you to my friend;
And you be not, hang, beg, starve, die in the streets

In *Romeo and Juliet*, this **patriarchal** dominance results in Juliet's tragic death; in *Much Ado About Nothing*, potential disaster is averted, and we therefore appreciate the play's cheerful resolution even more.

In addition to the thematic similarities between the comedies, the language of the plays also has a lot in common. Images of natural fertility and plenty abound (often associated with Aphrodite and Hymen, the gods of childbirth and marriage), particularly in the plays that have a visibly 'green' setting (for example, *As You Like It*). The language of hunting is also popular, often expressing a perception of romance as a game in pursuit of a piece of prey (i.e. a wife or husband).

The musical interludes in most comedies (for example, Borachio's song in Act II scene 3 of *Much Ado About Nothing*) emphasise the link between romance and musical harmony while providing an important opportunity to lighten the tone and break up the monotony of a long dramatic performance. This effect can also be achieved by the ubiquitous subplot featuring 'low' characters, like Dogberry and the Watch in *Much Ado About Nothing*. These scenes might have appealed to the 'groundlings' who paid the lowest price for admission to the theatre and stood in the 'pit' at the front of the stage in Shakespeare's time.

There are clearly striking similarities between Shakespeare's comedies, but students should be careful not to generalise too widely. Many critics take issue with the assumption that *Much Ado About Nothing* is a comic play with an unambiguously optimistic message. Twentieth-century commentators have lingered on the play's apparent sexism, Claudio's behaviour towards Hero, and Don Pedro's excessive interest in his friends' relationships to paint a sinister picture of Messinian society. When tackling issues surrounding **genre**, students should beware of categorising a play too narrowly; *Much Ado About Nothing* is most fascinating when its generic complexities are acknowledged and discussed rather than ignored or downplayed.

Play context

It is widely assumed that Shakespeare never left England, though the majority of his plays, in all **genres**, are set in other countries. Italy was particularly favoured because it was the origin of the **Renaissance** and home to many of the **source** texts that inspired Shakespeare and his contemporaries. Foreign settings also have the advantage of allowing comments on local political and social issues to be made circumspectly, as in *Measure for Measure*.

Shakespeare used known **sources** for 35 of his 37 plays, and it is assumed that the other two must have had sources as yet undiscovered. In this period, before and for some time after (until the emergence of the aptly named 'novel' **genre** in the early eighteenth century), originality of plot or character was not considered necessary, or even desirable, in literary works. A largely illiterate population and a traditional oral culture created a demand for the familiar and reassuring, as with children and their bedtime stories. Audiences already expected to know the basic storylines, settings and outcomes of plays they attended, and the skill and creativity of the playwright was demonstrated by the quality of the improvements they made to an existing work.

Much Ado About Nothing differs from many of Shakespeare's plays in that it does not have a single main **source**. Shakespeare drew heavily on Ludovico Ariosto's *Orlando Furioso* (1516, trans. 1591) for the Claudio/Hero plot, but he also made use of material from novella 22 of *La Prima Parte de la Novelle del Bandello* (usually referred to as *Bandello*, 1554), Edmund Spenser's *The Faerie Queene* (1596 edition) and the tale of *Fedele and Fortunio*, which is credited to Anthony Munday (1595).

The printed text

No manuscripts of any of Shakespeare's plays have survived. Some of the plays were published during his lifetime, in editions known as 'Quarto' because of the size of the paper used. In 1623, after his death, a collected edition known as the First Folio was published, containing all of his plays except *Pericles*. Although the Folio is generally considered to be more reliable than the Quartos, the authority or authenticity of any particular version of a play has to be assessed on its merits.

Much Ado About Nothing was probably first performed in 1598, and was originally published in the Quarto of 1600, before appearing in the Folio of 1623. There are few significant differences between the two texts, though a few minor errors from the Quarto are corrected in the Folio. Some of the punctuation is also amended in the Folio. There are still one or two contestable issues with regard to the text. For example, in Act II scene 1, lines 88, 91 and 93 of both the Quarto and the Folio editions are given to Benedick. As he speaks to Beatrice very shortly after this in a different context, this seems unlikely. Most editors therefore attribute them to Balthasar.

Whichever edition of the play you use, a number of changes will have been made from the original text. Different editors are likely to have different views and to arrive at different conclusions. The changes, and arguments for them, are usually indicated in the textual notes, but the goal of an editor is generally to produce an edition that makes sense when acted on the stage, rather than to give an account of all the possible interpretations of the play.

The play on stage

Much Ado About Nothing was probably first performed in 1598 and, according to subsequent accounts, was very well received. James I was such an admirer of the play that he ordered it to be performed at his daughter Elizabeth's wedding celebrations

in 1613. It has inspired two operas, several film adaptations, and a number of stage adaptations across the centuries. This impressive list of literary offshoots underlines the fact that the play has consistently enjoyed popularity in a number of different social and historical contexts.

Although pre-Restoration performances of *Much Ado About Nothing* are not well documented, a number of literary allusions from Shakespeare's contemporaries and immediate successors suggest that the play enjoyed a good level of public popularity. In Elizabethan times, plays often went by more than one name, and records from the time indicate that 'Benedicte and Betteris' was produced with some success during this period. This title suggests that the feuding couple were probably the principal attraction for audiences, as they remain today.

In line with the trend for reinventing Shakespeare's plays for a Restoration audience, *Much Ado About Nothing* received a significant makeover in the seventeenth century. William Davenant (or D'Avenant) combined it with *Measure for Measure* to create *The Law Against Lovers*, a piece that Samuel Pepys mentions in his diary of 1662 as 'a good play and well performed'. It largely follows the plot of *Measure for Measure*, while introducing the popular *Much Ado About Nothing* characters of Benedick and Beatrice to play the roles of Angelo's brother and Juliet's cousin respectively.

Like Davenant, Charles Johnson chose to combine *Much Ado About Nothing* with another Shakespearean comedy — *As You Like It* — to produce the hybrid play *Love in a Forest* in 1723, which featured lines from a number of Shakespeare's other works. James Miller's *The Universal Passion* (1737) likewise drew (though much less heavily than Davenant and Johnson) on the Benedick/Beatrice relationship in *Much Ado About Nothing*, but seems to have received little critical acclaim.

As with many of Shakespeare's works, these loose adaptations were popular during the seventeenth century and the first half of the eighteenth, but were gradually superseded by productions based on the original text as the eighteenth century progressed. By the time veteran Shakespeare actor David Garrick organised a Shakespeare jubilee in 1769, he had made the role of Benedick his own, revelling in the character's wit and word-play. He returned to the part at intervals for over 25 years, and the renaissance of *Much Ado About Nothing* seems to have owed a great deal to Garrick's popularity.

If Garrick's patronage of the play helped it accomplish popularity in the second half of the eighteenth century, it became even more established after 1800. The role of Beatrice became increasingly sought after by actresses of the period, and was taken by a string of excellent performers, most notably Helen Faucit and Ellen Terry. Between them they acted the part for over 65 years, developing Beatrice into a more complex and compassionate character than she had seemed before. Terry went on to deliver a series of lectures that explored the difficulties and successes of portraying a leading female character in the **patriarchal** world of the theatre.

The inescapable gender divide in the play has often informed directors' choice of setting. The cruel treatment of Hero has repeatedly been linked to the play's military backdrop, as the returning soldiers assert their masculine values on the women of the play. John Barton chose to set his 1976 production in nineteenth-century colonial India, thereby emphasising the role of the army in forming social networks and patterns of behaviour. Other productions have capitalised on the play's Sicilian setting by drawing attention to the island's modern connection to the Italian Mafia, and concepts of male honour and solidarity.

Much Ado About Nothing is a relatively short play, but it is also one of Shakespeare's most dynamic and varied when performed. It is loaded with dance, ceremony, visual entertainment and, most importantly, music. *Much Ado About Nothing* is one of Shakespeare's most melodic plays, and its songs and musical interludes serve to retain the audience's attention whenever the narrative drive slows down. The musical **metaphor** that runs through the drama also plays on ideas of discord and harmony, which were in common usage during the sixteenth and seventeenth centuries. Beatrice uses the vocabulary of dance as a means of exploring human relationships and it is significant that the characters return to the harmonious environment of the dance floor at the end of the play, having resolved the conflict engendered by Don John's malevolent plan.

The roles of Beatrice and Benedick are intrinsically linked, and it would be inadequate to discuss the different methods of approaching one role without considering the effect these would have on the other. Although many critics view the witty repartee between the two as the play's principal attraction, it should not be allowed to overshadow the Hero/Claudio marriage plot, as this can lead to a sense of deflation during the crucial church scene and its aftermath, when the tone of the play changes dramatically. Beatrice and Benedick have been played as middle aged, an interpretation that explains their more cynical approach to love and assured command of language, as well as providing a foil for the 'young love' enjoyed by Hero and Claudio. Perhaps the key issue when playing these parts is to decide how they interact with one another during their bantering exchanges. Is Beatrice, stung by a previous relationship with Benedick, bitter and acerbic in her put-downs, or do they represent a wry attempt at wooing him? Are Benedick's **misogynistic** musings a cover for flirtation, or do they reflect a deeply held belief in male gender superiority? Whichever of these readings is preferred, it will need to be compatible with the lovers' exchange in Act V scene 4, when the pair publicly declare their feelings for one another.

Claudio, like Hero, is a young lover, whose relative inexperience can be used by directors as mitigation for his abominable behaviour to Hero in the church scene. Others show him as an emotionally immature young soldier who takes the sexist jokes of his military comrades far too literally and applies them to his own dealings with women. A crucial directorial decision is whether or not to portray Borachio's balcony scene on stage. This opportunity for the audience to share in the

deception of Claudio has been used to evoke sympathy for the victim of a deviously well-executed plan, or as a means of underlining Claudio's gullibility.

Hero is the subject of others' speech throughout *Much Ado About Nothing*, but speaks few lines herself. Some early actors therefore played her as a submissive and colourless character who reacts with steadfast compliance to the male characters around her. She is markedly more spirited in the company of other women, and this aspect of her character is just as valid, particularly in the twenty-first century. An effective performance of Hero's role therefore depends as much on the way she reacts (physically and verbally) to others' opinions and actions as the way she delivers her own lines.

Minor characters also give scope for varying interpretations. Don John is usually played as a motiveless villain, with little complexity of character. However, some directors have suggested (as is the case in some of Shakespeare's **sources**) that his actions are fuelled by jealousy, and portray him as a lonely lover who pines for Hero in the very scenes in which he betrays her. The relationship between Don John and Don Pedro also allows for plenty of dramatic symmetry, reinforcing the literary tradition of two brothers who are opposed in morality and fortunes (as we see too in *Hamlet* and *King Lear*). **Ambiguity** is likewise built into Leonato's character. He can be shown as a benevolent father, weeping sorrowfully at Claudio's denunciation of Hero in Act IV scene 1, or an egotistical patriarch who is ready to believe common slander above the word of his own daughter. Other smaller parts, such as those of Borachio, Margaret, Conrade, Dogberry and the Friar are of primary importance to the development of the plot, but rarely take centre stage. As a result, the burden of dramatic tension shifts on to the more complex characters of Benedick and Beatrice, Claudio and Hero, upon whom the success of any production invariably depends.

Critical history

Early performances of *Much Ado About Nothing* are, as with many Shakespeare plays, not well documented. However, what little we know suggests that critics have historically found it to be one of Shakespeare's most sophisticated and enjoyable comedies.

In its earliest form, the play was sometimes titled or subtitled as 'Benedicte and Betteris' or 'Benedik and Betrice', indicating that the linguistic virtuosity of these two characters made them the chief sources of amusement for many theatre-goers. This view is propounded by Peter Hollindale, who goes so far as to suggest that 'compared with them, most other characters appear wooden and immobile'(in *Critical Essays on 'Much Ado About Nothing'* 1989). Claudio's macho behaviour was less problematic for early critics than more recent ones, and the multiple betrayal of Hero by the men of the play was likewise deemed more acceptable in Shakespeare's time, when an influential women's rights movement did not exist.

During the seventeenth century the play continued to enjoy great popularity, and it received an extra injection of life as it was revised for the stage by a number of eminent playwrights of the time. The Restoration rewritings of *Much Ado About Nothing* all combined the play with other Shakespearean dramas. However, the element most often borrowed from the text was once again the Beatrice/Benedick plot.

It took around a century for the original text to be restored to the stage in the majority of productions, after which point it was performed to significant acclaim. In 1795 Charles Dibdin asserted that *Much About About Nothing* 'is so witty, so playful, so abundant in strong writing, and rich humour, that it has always attracted universal applause'. Charlotte Lennox might have disagreed with this view, as in 1753 she had declared the play to be 'mangled and defaced, full of inconsistencies, contradictions and blunders'.

Although it was generally a popular hit, the play's female characters continued to suffer at the hands of the male-dominated establishment. In particular, many critics found Beatrice to be bitter and unpleasantly forthright rather than witty and vivacious. However, this view began to be challenged more seriously during the nineteenth century, as commentators considered the play's female roles in the context of growing unease over the institutional subjugation of women. Beatrice's cause was also aided by a series of excellent actresses who took on the role for a sustained period of time. Most notably, Helena Faucit and Ellen Terry worked hard to give the part depth, complexity and compassion, forcing a critical re-evaluation of Beatrice's motives and manners in performance. Terry's lectures on Shakespeare's women gave credence to a **feminist** account of the play. *The New York Times* in November 1910 reports how her lecture 'was greeted with obviously sincere warmth by a packed house of women, who had braved the torrents of rain in order to see and hear her. For half an hour before the matinée Forty-fourth Street was practically blocked with taxis, hansoms, and motor cars'.

In the twentieth century, the brutalising influence of two world wars drastically altered the way that critics and directors perceived the soldiers in the play, as did the success of the women's movement. For some critics, these developments infused the play with a depressing or sinister tone, while for others they added to the complexity of a comedy that has always been about 'the battle of the sexes'. *Much Ado About Nothing* was written when women's rights were virtually non-existent, but critics now find it increasingly difficult to reconcile Benedick's eloquent **misogyny** with a 'happy' ending to the play for Beatrice. As a result, many directors have either cut or toned down some of his more outrageous sexism. Hero's dilemma has likewise provided a focal point for political and feminist readings of the play up to the present day. Such **hermeneutic** difficulties have contributed to a groundswell of opinion that 'we might begin to think seriously about assigning *Much Ado About Nothing* to the category of "problem plays"' (Graham Holderness, in *Critical Essays on 'Much Ado*

About Nothing', 1989). There is an increasing focus on female characters in criticism of the play, and Beatrice appears to be one of the chief reasons for *Much Ado About Nothing*'s longevity of appeal. John Dover Wilson remarked in 1962 that 'Beatrice is the first woman in our literature, perhaps in the literature of Europe, who not only has a brain, but delights in the constant employment of it'. For Wilson and many others, she is a profoundly modern literary woman who has at last found a historical context in which she can be properly appreciated.

Much Ado About Nothing continues to capture the attention of critics and audiences; very few of Shakespeare's other comedies have been reinvigorated with such great success over a long period of time. Although it has not received as much exposure on the exam specifications as *Twelfth Night*, *A Midsummer Night's Dream* or *The Taming of the Shrew*, the play has nonetheless enjoyed great popularity as one of Shakespeare's most-performed comedies. Beatrice and Benedick's relationship in particular has helped the play achieve a timeless appeal, and the sheer linguistic richness of the play suggests that it will continue to do so. It offers opportunities for more sophisticated analysis than some of Shakespeare's more conventional comedies, and has a rich tradition of stimulating a variety of alternative readings, which makes it a rewarding and fruitful text to study.

Any play must be considered in relation to its historical, political and social background, and be viewed in the context of contemporary attitudes, however unconsciously they are drawn on. On the other hand, our critical interpretations should include responses to the issues that concern us nowadays, such as the stereo-typing of race and gender in the portrayal of women and different cultures from around the world. A **feminist** critique will try to ascertain whether the play challenges or accepts and endorses the **patriarchal** status quo and the **misogyny** of the time; **structuralist** approaches will look at language to expose the shifting and **ambivalent** relationship between words and meaning (signifier and signified); **post-structuralists** will look for what isn't there as well as what is, at how the plot is framed and at the assumptions being made within, and about, the play. A combi-nation of all of these critical approaches will produce essays that show an awareness of a range of reader responses and audience reactions, and that cover the examina-tion assessment criteria.

Scene summaries and notes

Act I scene 1

Don Pedro and his military party land in Messina, where they are entertained by Leonato, who plans a ball to celebrate their arrival. Beatrice and Benedick show their dislike for one another by exchanging caustic witticisms, before Claudio privately confesses to Benedick that he loves Leonato's daughter, Hero. As a sworn **misogynist**,

Benedick teases Claudio that Hero is unworthy of him. Don Pedro then enters and he and Claudio mock Benedick for his attitude to marriage. Benedick leaves, and Don Pedro agrees to approach Hero on Claudio's behalf to gain her hand in marriage.

From the outset of the play, there is a strong emphasis on the male characters' military background, and the importance of **patriarchal** society in Messina. There is a great deal of masculine joking, which is unflattering to women and **objectifies** them. These exchanges between Don Pedro, Claudio and Benedick hint that the men may be at odds with the courtly world of romance they are about to enter. Beatrice is ready to upset the conventions of society with her sharp tongue; the sexual and intellectual tension between her and Benedick is explored in their witty exchanges, and it is clear that they have a lot in common, despite the appearance of disagreement between them.

Many of the classic themes of comedy are introduced, as Benedick staunchly claims he will never marry (he will, of course, in comic tradition) and Claudio quickly falls in love. Don Pedro's promise to woo Hero on Claudio's behalf exemplifies the intricacies of the courtly system of love, whereby a suitor would be expected to win over both his beloved and her father before the marriage could take place. The fact that Claudio is delegating this job to his friend Don Pedro leaves open the possibility of miscommunication or betrayal, as we see in subsequent scenes.

Act I scene 2

Antonio passes on to his brother, Leonato, a message from an inept servant, who mistakenly believes that Don Pedro intends to woo Hero for himself at that evening's ball. Leonato decides to pass the news on to Hero.

This brief scene establishes the theme of misunderstanding and miscommunication that runs throughout the play. Although Leonato doubts what he has been told, he still considers the information reliable enough to pass on to his daughter. Such hearsay provides the foundation for most of the play's intrigue, as we see in later scenes.

Act I scene 3

Borachio informs Don John that Don Pedro intends to woo Hero on Claudio's behalf at the ball, and Don John celebrates the opportunity this provides for doing mischief.

In this scene, Don John proves himself to be the embodiment of the Elizabethan bastard — a character whose illegitimate birth manifests itself in his immoral behaviour. The first seeds of disruption in Messina are sown, and tension builds as we perceive the tragic potential of misunderstanding.

Act II scene 1

As the ball is about to start, Beatrice and Hero comment on how melancholy Don John looks, before Beatrice jokes about her unwillingness to marry. The dance begins, and the company put on their masks. Don Pedro takes Hero aside to present

Claudio's suit, and Beatrice takes advantage of her disguise to mock Benedick, pretending she thinks he is someone else.

Don John tries to disrupt the party by telling Claudio that Don Pedro is wooing Hero for himself. The confusion is soon ironed out, however, and Leonato offers Claudio his daughter's hand in marriage. Once Benedick and Beatrice have left, Don Pedro suggests a plan to trick Benedick and Beatrice into loving one another.

This scene is almost a **microcosm** of the play, full of flirtation, disguise, confusion and wit. We see Balthasar attempting to woo Margaret, and Ursula teasing Antonio, and there is a general mood of merriment, which emphasises the strong link between music and love in this scene. Nonetheless, Don John is a sinister presence throughout, and his manipulation almost succeeds in disrupting the engagement of Claudio and Hero.

The conflict between Beatrice and Bendick is at its height in this scene, and Benedick declares that he can hardly bear to be in the same room as her. Don Pedro's plan to bring the two together therefore adds a frisson to the interval between Claudio and Hero's engagement and their intended wedding in a week's time. However, Claudio himself is less enthusiastic about the delay to his nuptials, complaining that 'Time goes on crutches till love have all his rites' (330–31). Although the scene ends in a spirit of fun, Claudio's immaturity, and his earlier willingness to believe Don John's rumours, foreshadow his later gullibility.

Act II scene 2

Having heard that Claudio and Hero are to marry, Don John readily agrees to Borachio's plan for disrupting the wedding. Borachio explains that he will trick Claudio by wooing Hero's attendant, Margaret, at her mistress's window, giving the impression that he is wooing Hero herself. Delighted at this device, Don John leaves to find out when Claudio and Hero are due to be married.

The plot between Don John and Borachio adds an important element of **dramatic irony**, as none of the 'good' characters knows what is being planned. The audience feels a build-up of tension as we once again see the disruptive potential of deception and disguise.

Act II scene 3

Alone in the garden, Benedick muses on how Claudio's behaviour has been changed by love. As he hears Don Pedro, Leonato and Claudio approach, Benedick hides and listens to their conversation. Knowing that Benedick is listening to them, the three friends talk loudly about how much Beatrice is in love with him. The group then go in to dinner, while Benedick mulls over what he has heard. He decides to requite Beatrice's love, and interprets her rudeness as an expression of affection when she comes to summon him for dinner.

The gulling of Benedick provides a benign comic parallel to Don John's deception of Claudio. Both characters are willing to believe the rumours spread by others, though one makes himself a figure of fun while the other almost causes a tragedy. This time we see the comic potential for **dramatic irony** as we witness Benedick's swift conversion from cynic to lover. The link between music and love is once again emphasised by Balthasar's song in this scene, and his famous line 'Men were deceivers ever' (61) contradicts Benedick's usual complaint that women are unfaithful, thus mirroring Benedick's change of heart regarding Beatrice. The exchange between Beatrice and Benedick at the end of the scene emphasises the central theme in the play that people see what they want to see, or hear what they want to hear. Benedick reads a 'double meaning' (250) into Beatrice's unambiguously brusque remark 'Against my will I am sent to bid you come in to dinner' (239–40), thus providing another amusing case of miscommunication in the play.

Act III scene 1

On Hero's instruction, Margaret brings Beatrice to the garden in order to overhear a conversation between Hero and Ursula. While Beatrice eavesdrops, Hero bewails the fact that Benedick is in love with so proud a woman as her cousin. Hero then tells Ursula that she will try to convince Benedick to take his love elsewhere, to save himself the pain of rejection. Hero and Ursula exit, celebrating their deceit, and the scene ends with Beatrice promising to requite Benedick's love.

The gulling of Beatrice is almost identical to the deception of Benedick in Act II scene 3, and highlights how similar the two of them are. Hero and her companions repeatedly use the imagery of angling and trapping in this scene, once again emphasising how trickery can be used to bring people together, rather than part them as Don John attempts to do. After listening to Hero's unflattering description of her pride, Beatrice undergoes a change of heart, which is almost as startling as Benedick's. It seems that both characters have been at least subconsciously aware of their feelings for one another, and the 'traps' (106) set by Cupid have finally ensnared them simultaneously.

Act III scene 2

After his gulling in Act II scene 3, Benedick is no longer his usual self. Ashamed to admit he is sighing for love of Beatrice, he tells Don Pedro and Claudio that he has toothache. His companions point out that he has shaved his beard and brushed his hat; under the pressure of this teasing, Benedick excuses himself to speak to Leonato. Don John now enters and offers Claudio proof that Hero has been unfaithful to him. The scene ends with both Claudio and Don Pedro swearing to disgrace Hero on her wedding day if the allegations are true.

At first, Benedick seems to want to discuss his change of heart with his friends, declaring 'I am not as I have been' (14). However, the teasing of Claudio and Don Pedro forces him to hide his feelings in the pretence that he has 'the toothache' (20). This exchange once again makes use of **dramatic irony** for comic effect, as we laugh at Benedick's inability

to express his true feelings for Beatrice. The mood of the scene quickly shifts away from light-hearted comedy when Don John arrives. In stark contrast to the tone of Act II scene 3 and Act III scene 1, he uses the persuasive power of **rhetoric** for evil means. Claudio is worryingly quick to accept the accusations levelled at his betrothed, and this emphasises his youth and inexperience. At the start of the scene Don Pedro describes marriage as a new outfit that Claudio must be as eager as a child to try on. This comparison is fitting, as Claudio shows a naïve and impressionable nature, which Don John exploits when he speaks of Hero's infidelity.

Act III scene 3

Officer Dogberry assembles the city Watch, dispensing hilariously bad advice to his men. He retires for the night, asking to be woken if any serious incident arises. The watchmen then overhear Borachio boasting to Conrade of the money he has earned by betraying Hero. Although the watchmen do not understand the extent of Borachio's villainy, they take the two men away for questioning.

This is the first scene in the play that revolves around characters from the Messinian lower classes, with all their foibles and failings. As we see in the two gulling scenes, eavesdropping is an important plot device, as Borachio's inability to conceal his deceit proves his undoing here. The problems of communication are brought into sharp relief by the watchmen's incomprehension and Dogberry's frequent use of **malapropisms**. Although we are pleased to see Borachio apprehended at the end of this scene, the bungling of the watchmen means that we cannot be sure his plot will be discovered in time to avert disaster.

Act III scene 4

It is Hero's wedding day, and she compares different outfits with Margaret. Beatrice then enters, claiming to feel ill, and Margaret jokes that she must be in love. As the scene ends, Hero's wedding party is approaching to take her to church.

Given the plot described by Borachio in the previous scene, our enjoyment of Hero's wedding preparations is tempered with a sense of uncertainty about what will happen when she reaches the church. Nonetheless, Margaret's teasing of Beatrice hits a comic note. Beatrice's so-called illness reminds us of Benedick's 'toothache' in Act III scene 2, underlining the similarity between the two characters, and contributes to the sense of a developing love affair. Margaret is revealed as an earthy and sexually outspoken woman in this scene, teasing Hero about her wedding night in a risqué manner. These exchanges serve to emphasise Hero's own purity, and cast a doubt over Margaret's morality (particularly in light of the fact that Borachio implicated her in his plot).

Act III scene 5

Dogberry informs Leonato about the arrest of Borachio and Conrade, but his longwinded prattle irritates Leonato, who is in a rush to get to Hero's wedding.

Leonato ends up leaving before the plot has been revealed, asking Dogberry to question the suspects and bring the report to him afterwards.

This short scene builds a great deal of tension, as Leonato narrowly misses out on preventing Hero's public humiliation in Act IV scene 1. Once again, Dogberry's use of absurd and inaccurate language reminds us of the communication gap between characters and classes, and the tragic potential of misunderstanding.

Act IV scene 1

During the wedding service Claudio publicly disgraces Hero by accusing her of infidelity. Despite her denials, Don Pedro joins in the denunciation. Hero then faints in shock as Don Pedro, Don John and Claudio storm out. Believing the accusation against his daughter, Leonato prays that she will die in order to hide her shame. Benedick tries to calm Leonato down, whilst Beatrice asserts that her cousin has been betrayed. The Friar then interjects, declaring his belief that Hero is innocent. Benedick suggests that Don John may be responsible for having misled Claudio and Don Pedro. At this, Leonato declares that he will kill Hero if she has been deceitful, or Don John and his followers if they are proved to have slandered Hero unjustly.

The Friar then suggests that, as Hero is assumed to be dead, Leonato should organise a memorial service at the family monument. In the meantime, the Friar thinks that Claudio will repent the actions that led to his sweetheart's apparent death. If her name is subsequently cleared, the lovers can be reunited; if not, then Hero can secretly go to a nunnery.

Beatrice and Benedick are left alone as the others go to execute the Friar's plan. Benedick comforts Beatrice, and they declare their love to one another. Beatrice then asks Benedick to show his love by killing Claudio. Benedick initially refuses, but finally agrees to challenge his friend to a duel, and leaves to do so.

This is the play's pivotal moment, when the plot reaches crisis point and the actions of each character reveal their true colours. The **misogyny** latent in Messina combines with Don John's manipulative tactics to threaten the city's social order and make plain the gender conflict at its heart.

Leonato's disownment of his daughter is a shocking and poignant moment which reveals his weakness of character and exceeds even the cruelty of Don Pedro and Claudio. Since he is her father and protector, it is appalling to see him turn on her so viciously in the absence of any substantial proof against her. In contrast, Benedick breaks with the **patriarchal** code of his male friends and sides with Beatrice. This is a benchmark of how far he has come in the play, as he agrees to challenge Claudio in order to defend the honour of a woman. His decision to trust Beatrice's judgement shows the uniting power of unconditional love, faith and trust. Even the wordplay between the two has softened by this point in the play, and their **punning** is tinged with sorrow and tenderness. The Friar's intervention, as a man of faith and morality, reassures us that the pair are right to defend Hero's honour.

In the midst of all this drama, we are reminded of the remarkable ill fortune that allows Borachio and Don John's plot to work so well. The improbable success of their plan is illustrated by Beatrice's claim that she spent only one night in the last year away from Hero — which happens to be the one on which Hero is accused of having betrayed Claudio. In the absence of any solid evidence for or against Hero, Shakespeare thus forces his characters to follow their true beliefs.

Act IV scene 2

Dogberry conducts the interrogation of Borachio and Conrade in his usual verbose and clumsy style. He finally elicits a confession, which the Sexton takes to Leonato. We also learn that Don John has fled Messina.

This potentially comic scene is penetrated by a sense of tension as we are by now acutely aware of the consequences of the truth being concealed. Once again, Dogberry's self-importance contrasts with his role as a public servant, and his ineptitude contributes to our anxiety that Borachio's confession be heard before any more damage is caused.

Act V scene 1

Leonato turns his anger away from Hero and towards her accusers, as he and Antonio challenge Claudio to a duel in order to prove Hero's innocence. Claudio refuses the challenge, and Don Pedro stands up for his friend, reiterating that Hero is guilty.

Leonato and Antonio leave the scene, and Benedick enters with another challenge for Claudio. Claudio jokingly ignores it, and he and Don Pedro proceed to tease Benedick about Beatrice. As Benedick leaves, he reveals, much to Don Pedro's discomfort, that Don John has fled Messina. Dogberry, Verges and the Watch then arrive, and Borachio confesses his villainy. Leonato enters and both Claudio and Don Pedro beg forgiveness for their actions. Leonato commands them to spread word of Hero's innocence around Messina, and tells Claudio to write an epitaph in Hero's memory. Finally, Leonato tells Claudio that he must marry Leonato's (fictional) niece, as a form of repentance. Claudio agrees to all these terms. As Claudio exits to mourn at Hero's memorial, Leonato goes to question Margaret about her part in Borachio's plot.

Seemingly in shock over the revelations of Act IV scene 1, Leonato shows his contradictory feelings towards Hero as he alternates between disdain for her and wrath towards her accusers. His moral code has been thrown into turmoil, and he seems to be on the verge of a nervous breakdown at the start of the scene. Claudio and Don Pedro's behaviour is even more disconcerting, as they continue to crack jokes with one another, despite the news that Hero is dead. This unflattering depiction of Hero's closest friends is brought into sharp relief by Benedick's calm and principled challenge to Claudio, which is once more met with a barrage of inappropriate jokes. When it comes, the revelation of Hero's innocence begins the play's **dénouement**, and changes the tone of the scene dramatically. Don Pedro and Claudio are finally made to show humility, and the tension caused by Dogberry's ineptitude is released as he is despatched with a reward for his troubles.

Act V scene 2

Benedick calls to see Beatrice, and Margaret makes him promise to write her a sonnet if she lets him in to see his sweetheart. When Beatrice enters, she demands to know the outcome of Benedick's challenge to Claudio, and refuses to kiss him when she learns that they did not fight. She relents when Benedick explains that he is awaiting Claudio's response to his challenge. The couple then resume their wordplay, before Ursula rushes in with news of Hero's innocence. Beatrice and Benedick depart, to hear the news in full at Leonato's house.

This short scene continues to develop Beatrice and Benedick's relationship, and shows the depth of their affection for one another. Unlike Claudio and Hero, the pair know each other well, and enjoy a genuine intellectual connection. Their exchanges are no longer punctuated by brazen insults, and their banter now suggests a meeting of minds rather than a conflict of interests. Benedick shows how much he has changed by attempting to sing a love song while he waits for Beatrice, and his observation that 'Thou and I are too wise to woo peaceably' (66) reminds us that their attraction to one another is based on the outspoken wit they share.

Act V scene 3

Claudio reads his epitaph at Hero's memorial, and swears to repeat the rite annually. Don Pedro then suggests that they change out of their mourning clothes before going to Leonato's house.

Claudio's tribute to Hero is crucial to the play's successful **dénouement**, and paves the way for the couple's happy reunion. His clothes and words provide important visual evidence of his repentance, and increase our anticipation of the revelation that Hero is actually still alive. Claudio ends the scene by invoking Hymen, the god of marriage, in the hope that future love affairs end more happily; his request is answered in the very next scene.

Act V scene 4

This final scene begins with the Friar happily proclaiming Hero's innocence and Leonato exonerating Claudio and Don Pedro for their actions. Leonato then instructs all the ladies to withdraw and put on their masks. As the remaining men wait for Claudio and Don Pedro's arrival, Benedick successfully asks Leonato for his

niece's hand in marriage. Don Pedro and Claudio now enter, and Claudio agrees to marry Hero's masked 'cousin'. Instead, Hero unveils herself and the two lovers are reunited. In the ensuing excitement, Claudio and Hero produce sonnets that they have stolen from Beatrice and Benedick, expressing their feelings for one another. The pair finally admit their love publicly and Benedick suggests a celebratory dance before the weddings take place. Finally, a messenger enters with the news that Don John has been captured.

Superficially at least, an aura of reconciliation and peace pervades the scene, as wrongs are forgiven and love overcomes adversity. Shakespeare employs **dramatic irony** once more, clothing Hero in the play's final disguise before she reveals herself to Claudio, thereby restoring equilibrium to Messina. Beatrice and Benedick must also confront their faults by abandoning their pride, publicly admitting their feelings for one another, and acknowledging the change they have undergone by falling in love. Finally, Don John's capture imparts a sense of **poetic justice** and closure to the play before the curtain falls. Benedick's suggestion of a dance is a particularly fitting celebration as order and harmony return to the stage.

Characters

Dramatis personae

Don Pedro is the prince of Arragon, and Leonato's most distinguished guest. He is older than Claudio and Benedick (who are described as 'young'). His high social standing seems to rule him out of a marriage to any of Messina's women, and he instead contents himself with matchmaking for others.

Leonato is the governor of Messina, Hero's father and Beatrice's guardian. He mentions his wife early in the play, but she never appears on stage. Leonato seems socially ambitious in his desire to marry Hero to Claudio or Don Pedro.

Hero is Leonato's daughter, named after the tragic character in Greek mythology, who committed suicide after her lover Leander died. Like the name Desdemona (meaning 'unfortunate') in *Othello*, Hero's name hints that she will be mistreated in the play. She is a chaste, modest and beautiful woman, whose hand in marriage is sought by Claudio. We are repeatedly reminded of her youth, and her fate is largely decided by the male characters around her.

Beatrice is Leonato's niece, and has grown up in her uncle's care after being orphaned at an early age. These events indicate that she has already experienced loss, and it is hinted that she has been romantically involved with Benedick, and hurt by him, in the past. Known to Benedick as 'Lady Disdain' (I.1.110) and 'Lady Tongue' (II.1.252), she has developed a habit of hiding her feelings behind her cutting wit.

She is forthright and outspoken, and is loyal in defence of her friends. Her name translates as 'she who gives blessings', which links her to Benedick.

Benedick is described in the cast list as a 'young lord', though he is sometimes played as a character in his late 30s or early 40s. He has returned from war with a fine military reputation, and is also renowned for his wordplay. His name comes from the Latin for 'blessed' and translates as 'well spoken' or 'fine speaker', as befits a man with a good command of language. His name alliterates with Beatrice's, and has the same etymological root, linking the two as potential lovers.

Claudio is a young nobleman of Florence, who has just returned from war with his close friends Benedick and Don Pedro. He has served with distinction in the recent military conflict, but his youth suggests he is inexperienced and naive.

Don John is Don Pedro's bastard brother, who has recently been involved in a military action against his sibling. Although he seems to lack any tangible motive for his evil actions, he may well be driven by jealousy and bitter resentment of a society that looks down on those like him who are conceived out of wedlock.

Margaret is one of Hero's attendants. She is a socially ambitious woman of spirit and overt sexuality, whose liaisons with her lover Borachio result in Hero's disgrace in Act IV scene 1.

Dogberry is an inept but well-meaning constable who is in charge of the Watch. He is pompous, preoccupied with procedure and not as intelligent as he thinks he is; he constantly uses **malapropisms** without realising it.

The 'merry' war: Beatrice and Benedick

The relationship between Beatrice and Benedick has captured the imagination of audiences for centuries, and is still the most engaging element of *Much Ado About Nothing* for many critics. Differences of opinion have arisen, however, regarding the correct way of interpreting the characters. The actress Helena Faucit famously described the role of Beatrice as being 'charged with no real malice', while others have agreed with Benedick's description of her in the text as a **'harpy'** (II.1.248).

Although the Claudio/Hero plot is technically the play's central story, the relationship between Beatrice and Benedick has more depth, complexity and enduring appeal. When Shakespeare's play first appeared on stage, it was known **colloquially** by the names of the two lovers, and both characters proved so popular that they were exported into other comic plays (see, for example, Davenant's *The Law Against Lovers*, 1662). Hector Berlioz was so inspired by their story that he wrote an opera based on it, entitled *Béatrice et Bénédict* (1862). In many ways, the two lovers have come to represent the now familiar archetype of the sparring partners, whose attraction to one another manifests itself in mocking wit and **faux** dislike.

The thin line between love and hate

From the outset of the play, it is clear that Beatrice does not hold Benedick in high regard, at least not publicly. She accuses him of cowardice and gluttony, deliberately **punning** on the meaning of 'stomach' to suggest that he would rather eat than fight on the battlefield (I.1.46–48). She proceeds to call him fickle in his friendships, claiming that 'he hath every month a new sworn brother' (I.1.66–67), and that he smothers those he tries to befriend ('he will hang upon him like a disease', I.1.79).

Although some of the insults Beatrice throws at Benedick seem to be convenient one-liners rather than reflections of deeply held sentiments, some of her comments betray a genuine anger at his behaviour. This could be linked to her comment in Act I scene 1 that 'I know you of old' (136–37). She confesses to Don Pedro that Benedick once won her heart 'with false dice' (II.1.257), and much of the venom she directs against him may therefore be the result of a painful experience with him in the past.

Benedick's complaints about Beatrice tend to cite her contemptuous attitude towards him (calling her 'Lady Disdain', I.1.110) and her ceaseless talking (he refers to her as 'Lady Tongue', II.1.252). In a society where women were usually seen and not heard, Beatrice constitutes an awkward interlocutor, because Benedick does not want to lose face by being publicly outwitted by a woman, and yet he cannot address her gallantly, as noblemen were expected to do. As an attack upon her talkativeness he calls her 'a rare parrot-teacher' (I.1.130), though her wit often surpasses his own in originality and intellectual force.

Perhaps more significantly, most of Benedick's disparaging comments are aimed at women in general rather than at Beatrice herself. In Act I scene 1 he describes himself as 'a professed tyrant to their sex' (158–59), and repeatedly reinforces the claim he makes at the start of the play that 'I will live a bachelor' (I.1.226–27). Benedick also makes repeated reference to the cuckold's horns (see, for example, I.1.242–44), suggesting that he fears being made a fool by an unfaithful wife, and that this insecurity fuels his **misogynistic** sentiments. Tellingly, Benedick claims that Beatrice is more beautiful than Hero (I.1.178–80). Unlike Claudio and Hero, Beatrice and Benedick engage in lively social intercourse, which reveals how well matched they are intellectually, and despite their bickering there is an obvious sexual tension between them.

The balance of power between Beatrice and Benedick seems to change at various points within the play. At the end of the gulling scene in which Beatrice's feelings are made known to him, Benedick's self-confidence and vanity are reflected in his assumption that there must therefore be a 'double meaning' in her grudging invitation to dinner (II.3.250), and in his statement that he would be 'a villain' not to 'take pity of her' (II.3.253–54). In contrast, after the parallel gulling scene concerning Benedick's secret love, Beatrice admits her reciprocal feelings for him, but qualifies her joy with the condition that 'If thou dost love, my kindness shall incite thee / To bind our loves up in a holy band' (III.1.113–14). The word 'If' reflects a lingering insecurity on Beatrice's part about the truth of Benedick's feelings, and it is clear that she hopes the relationship will lead quickly to marriage ('holy band'), again possibly revealing her doubts about his trustworthiness.

An alternative interpretation of this scene is that it demonstrates Beatrice's prudence, and at times she does seem to have greater control over her feelings and the relationship. In Act IV scene 1 she meets Benedick's spontaneous confession 'I do love nothing in the world so well as you' (264) with a reticent answer: 'I confess nothing, nor I deny nothing. I am sorry for my cousin' (268–69). The implication is that in such a crisis there is no time for romantic sweet-talk, and that if Benedick wants to prove his love he must do so through action, not words, by duelling with Claudio. At the end of the play, however, it is Benedick's turn to curtail *her* talking. In their final exchange he commands 'Peace! I will stop your mouth', and kisses her (V.4.97). The play therefore ends with the assertion of masculine authority, but without creating the impression that Beatrice has been cowed. Although the 'merry war' has ended in a truce, the expectation is that affectionate sparring between this evenly matched couple will continue after marriage.

Leonato: doting father?

Critical opinion about Leonato is often divided between those who consider him a self-seeking social climber, and those who see him as a well-meaning father whose judgement of character is poor. Although he doesn't speak as much as some of the other characters in *Much Ado About Nothing*, his role as governor of Messina makes him central to the play's environment and therefore its outcome.

One of the first things that will strike audiences of *Much Ado About Nothing* is Leonato's elaborate use of language. He speaks more **verse** than anyone else in the play, marking him out as an affected and deliberate speaker. Verse is not a realistic mode of speech, and Leonato can often be seen using it on formal occasions (for example, during the church scene in Act IV scene 1), or when he is keen to assert his dignity and status (for example, when he challenges Claudio in Act V scene 1), thereby conveying his age, social status and level of education. Even when he speaks in prose, Leonato's language is carefully constructed to evoke a particular response in his audience. Speaking to Don Pedro when he arrives in Act I scene 1, Leonato's language is obviously designed to flatter, as he asserts, 'Never came trouble to my house in the likeness of your grace; for trouble being gone, comfort should remain; but when you depart from me sorrow abides and happiness takes his leave' (92–95). This longwinded speech essentially means 'It's nice to see you'. However, his mode of address ('your grace') is obsequious, and the use of personification ('sorrow' and 'happiness') is a poetic technique designed to emphasise Leonato's regard for the prince. Compare this speech to Leonato's blunt exchanges with the socially inferior Dogberry in Act III scene 5!

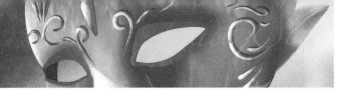

If Leonato is deferential to Don Pedro and the Prince's followers, he is more dominant in his dealings with Hero and, to a lesser extent, Beatrice. In Elizabethan times, it was the duty of a man to take on the raising of his brother's or sister's child if they lost their father. However, Leonato's treatment of Beatrice is quite different to that of his own daughter. At the start of the masked ball, Leonato keeps close control of Hero, instructing her in how to behave: 'Daughter, remember what I told you. If the Prince do solicit you in that kind, you know your answer' (II.1.58–60). In contrast, his parental authority melts away when addressing Beatrice, and he can only comment that 'niece, I hope one day to see you fitted with a husband.' (50–51). Even when Beatrice makes some ill-judged jokes about Don Pedro's single status in Act II scene 1, Leonato feels unable to reprimand her publicly, instead shooing her off the stage by asking 'Niece, will you look to those things I told you of?' (311–12). Leonato may well feel less comfortable disciplining his niece than his daughter, as they are not as closely related. Alternatively, as a proud patriarch he may be unwilling to confront a woman whose witty replies are likely to make him look intellectually inferior. Whatever the reason for his attitudes to the two young women, it is clear that Leonato offers his daughter much less freedom than his niece.

As Hero's father, Leonato is responsible for finding her a worthy husband. Attitudes to marriage were quite different in Shakespeare's time from what they are today (see *A courtly marriage*, pp. 43–45), and Leonato's behaviour should therefore be judged in the light of his own cultural context. He is certainly assiduous in preparing Hero for a proposal, telling her how to answer Don Pedro, should the Prince approach her at the masked ball. When he discovers Claudio's interest he is equally quick to seize the opportunity, accepting the proposal through Don Pedro without including Claudio in the discussion at all. Nonetheless, Claudio seems to be an impressive marriage prospect. He is a handsome man of good birth from an important city (Florence), with a fine military reputation. Perhaps the most worrying aspect of Leonato's behaviour is his readiness to marry Hero to Claudio even after she has been publicly disgraced by him. Leonato is very quick to forgive the man whom he had challenged to a duel, as if he wishes to capitalise on Claudio's sense of guilt and push the union through as quickly as possible. Although Leonato is acutely aware of the social implications of joining his family with Claudio's, it could be argued that by today's standards his indifferent attitude to the lord's personal qualities threaten Hero's chances of enjoying a fulfilling marriage.

Hero or zero?

Women are often at the centre of Shakespeare's plots, and yet they are rarely given the same number of lines as their male counterparts, nor have the same influence in their respective societies. Fathers and husbands are obsessed by their daughters'

and wives' chastity, their beauty and decorum, and yet we rarely hear the candid thoughts of women in a male-dominated society. Hero, like so many female characters in the **Renaissance** theatre, has a subtle and complex influence on the action of *Much Ado About Nothing*, and has been interpreted in a number of different ways over the years.

Although it is difficult to define her own character clearly, Hero acts as a useful mirror of others' values. The behaviour of her father, suitor, cousin and friends towards her reveals a great deal about them: her dutiful demeanour contrasts with Leonato's domineering and self-seeking nature; her beauty and chastity reflect Claudio's superficiality, suspicion and insecurity; her simple goodness brings out Beatrice's kindness, compassion and loyalty; the same quality causes Benedick to renounce his scepticism of women and offer her, and Beatrice, his trust.

In this sense, Hero's importance goes far beyond the lines that she speaks. She is the enigma at the centre of the play, who is both a symbol of female values and a social icon whom others struggle to control.

The goddess within

Hero's name derives from Greek mythology, which Christopher Marlowe used as a **source** for his poem *Hero and Leander*. This Hero was a priestess of Aphrodite (the goddess of love), who lived in the city of Sestos. Her lover Leander lived in the city of Abydos, which was separated from Sestos by a dangerous stretch of water called the Hellespont. Every night, Hero would light a torch in her tower to guide Leander as he swam across the strait to see her. One night, a storm blew out the torch, and Leander lost his way. When his drowned body washed up on the shore, Hero saw it and committed suicide by throwing herself out of the tower.

The Hero of Greek mythology is, like Shakespeare's character, a beautiful and noble woman. She is often seen as a symbol of romantic loyalty, as she is unable to carry on living once her lover is dead. This is paralleled in Shakespeare's decision to make his Hero steadfastly loyal to Claudio, despite his unjust accusation of her. She also suffers a mock 'death' in Act IV scene 1, which symbolises her inability to live longer than her relationship to Claudio. This scene highlights the play's tragic potential, as we wonder if Shakespeare's character will meet the same end as her Greek counterpart. Nonetheless, the tone of Shakespeare's work is fundamentally different from that of the myth, and we are left with a comic 'happy' ending rather than a tragic death when the curtain falls.

Benedick also makes a reference to Hero's Greek lover in Act V scene 2, as he states that 'in loving, Leander the good swimmer [...was...] never so truly turned over and over as my poor self in love' (30–31, 34–35). In doing so, he draws a parallel between the trials Leander faces to be with his lover, and Benedick's own struggle to swallow his pride and secure a future with Beatrice.

All these allusions would have been particularly relevant to Shakespeare's audiences, as Marlowe's poem *Hero and Leander* was written in 1598, the same year as *Much Ado About Nothing* was written.

What's in a name?

The word 'hero' can mean a number of different things. In theatrical terms it refers to a character who is at the centre of the narrative. Although Hero does not speak as many lines as other characters, she is the focus of much attention in Messinian society, whether people's intentions regarding her are good or bad.

The word 'hero' also suggests a character who possesses noble qualities like honour and integrity. Inner nobility was often linked to outer beauty, a connection to which Claudio refers when he disgraces Hero in Act IV scene 1. In lines 98–100, he complains:

> O Hero! What a Hero hadst thou been,
> If half thy outward graces had been placed
> About thy thoughts and counsels of thy heart!

In fact, Claudio is mistaken in his judgement of Hero's character, and her goodness is truly reflected in her appearance.

The idea of heroes being near-perfect (but often fatally flawed) specimens of humankind also comes from Greek mythology. Early in the play Claudio worships Hero almost as an idol or a symbol of perfection; his disillusionment when he believes that she has betrayed him is as excessive as his original estimation of her as a paragon. In fact, she proves too worthy of his adulation, showing personal virtue so far above normal human levels that it fulfils the notion of heroism as 'superhuman'.

Seen and not heard

There are several key passages in the play when Hero is on stage but silent. In Act I scene 1, she is on stage for some 150 lines, and speaks only one of them, even though Don Pedro refers to her in conversation with Leonato (96–97). From the outset of the play we are therefore shown her modesty and obedience in society, as she fulfils the model of the quiet and demure daughter.

In Act II scene 1 the ball is just about to start, and Hero makes mention of Don John's 'melancholy disposition' (5). However she is then silent until Don Pedro approaches her to dance in line 77, despite the fact that the other characters joke and discuss her love life in front of her. Even when Antonio says to her in lines 44–45, 'I trust you will be ruled by your father' (regarding the possibility of Don Pedro proposing to her), Beatrice replies in her cousin's place, asserting 'Yes, faith; it is my cousin's duty to make curtsy and say, "Father, as it please you"' (46–47). By speaking in such a cheeky and unconventional way Beatrice tries to represent her cousin's interests, when Hero is less willing to break the bounds of female social propriety by speaking in male company.

Hero's silence in these scenes and others reflects her obedience to the social code that women were to be 'seen and not heard'. However, her behaviour also has unfortunate consequences for others' perception of her. In fact, her quietness causes anxiety and mistrust in the male characters around her, even as it fulfils their demand for female obedience. Hero's silence makes it difficult for others (particularly men) to get to know her, and she is therefore something of an enigma to them. As soon as Hero leaves the stage in Act I scene 1, Claudio asks Benedick, 'Is she not a modest young lady?' (155), as if inferring that he cannot tell what she is like because he has not heard her speak (and, by implication that he is also unable to work out if she is as sexually modest as her demeanour suggests). In the absence of any real knowledge about his fiancée, Claudio is therefore susceptible to the rumours that circulate about her.

Though she says little herself, Hero is often the subject of others' conversation when she is off stage. Don John in particular is acutely aware of Hero's vulnerability to rumour in a society in which she does not have the authority to speak in her own defence. His ploy to disgrace Hero depends on the assumption that Claudio will not ask his fiancée about the allegations against her before he denounces her; sadly, Don John is proved correct. Just as Hero's honour is ruined by words spoken behind her back, Antonio and Leonato attempt to repair her reputation in the same way. In Act V scene 1, they both challenge Claudio to a duel in order to prove her honesty on the man who has denounced her. However, both characters fail to see the **irony** that Hero's misery has been created by exactly this sort of masculine exchange, where pride and honour are deemed more important than the truth.

Most poignantly, Claudio's **elegy** in Act V scene 3 is spoken when Hero's absence is most obvious in the play. Thinking his fiancée is dead, Claudio publicly declares his regret for his part in her demise. At last, Hero is a beneficiary rather than a victim of the words spoken in her absence, and the stage is set for a happy ending. Some directors even have Hero listening to the poem, unseen, so that she can see her future husband repent before she agrees to marry him.

Girl power

Given her obedient nature in the company of men, it is perhaps easier to get a sense of Hero's real personality when she is in the company of woman alone. In Act III scene 1 (the gulling of Beatrice) and Act III scene 4 (Hero's wedding preparations), we see Hero in the company of other women, and therefore free of the usual male strictures regarding her language and behaviour. In Act III scene 1, we see her as a more authoritative member of the ruling classes, as she uses imperative forms of verbs to issue commands to her servants ('Margaret, run thee to the parlour' (1); 'Whisper her [Beatrice's] ear' (4); 'leave us alone' (13), and so on). Throughout the gulling of Beatrice, Hero comes across as a witty, cheeky and likeable character, who enters into the tricking of her cousin with a warm-hearted sense of humour. She is once again amongst women as she prepares for her wedding in Act III scene 4.

Although she is able to speak more freely in the absence of men, she retains her sense of sexual modesty here, blushing at Margaret's crude joke about sex (24–25) and calling her maid a 'fool' (10). She is also complicit in Margaret's baiting of Beatrice, whom she teases about her lovesickness for Benedick. These two scenes shed important light on Hero's character, revealing a depth, complexity and humour that she does not feel able to display in male company

Claudio: 'Count Comfect'

Claudio has long been a problematic character for critics of *Much Ado About Nothing*. He is the archetype of the courtly lover, a handsome young lord with money and prospects, who would have been perceived as an ideal husband in his time. However, as centuries have passed, audiences have become more and more uncomfortable with his role and actions in the play. Beatrice's choice of the word 'Comfect' (meaning 'confectionery' or 'sweet') to describe Claudio reflects her view that his initially sweet and pleasant demeanour belies the cruelty of his behaviour to Hero. Claudio's motivations, weaknesses and virtues have been examined time and again to justify his actions or contradict the view that he is a worthy husband for Hero. The complexity of Claudio's character is all the more important for students to consider, given that he as at the heart of the play's main plot and its 'happy' ending.

Initially, Claudio seems to be a considerate suitor, claiming in Act I scene 1 that he does not wish to rush into a relationship with Hero: 'lest my liking might too sudden seem, / I would have salved it with a longer treatise' (293–94). Nonetheless, he decides to woo Hero despite having barely heard her speak. It is therefore unsurprising that Claudio's attraction for Hero is, at least partly, superficial. Referring to her good looks, Claudio asserts that 'In mine eye she is the sweetest lady that ever I looked on' (I.1.175–76). He clearly considers her desirable and decorative, like a 'jewel' (169) that others admire, and one that can be possessed like a trophy. Indeed, Claudio's most important criterion for his future wife seems to be the esteem in which his male companions hold her. After declaring his feelings for Hero, Claudio asks Benedick to 'speak in sober judgement' of her (160), before repeating the request once again: 'I pray thee tell me truly how thou likest her' (166–67). When Don Pedro arrives, Claudio is frightened that his friend is recommending Hero as a joke ('You speak this to fetch me in, my lord', 206), and only declares his final intention to marry once Don Pedro has declared 'she is worthy, I know' (212). Along with her beauty, it is crucial to Claudio that his wife is 'a modest lady' (I.1.155), and he is likewise concerned to find out whether Leonato has a son (273); if not, Hero will be Leonato's heir, and an even more attractive marital prospect.

There is also evidence that Claudio is an impressionable character, whose behaviour can be unpredictable. In Act II scene 3, Benedick marvels at Claudio's swift change from soldier to lover, using a musical **metaphor** to describe his change of taste from the soldier's 'drum and the fife' (14) to the lover's 'tabor and pipe'

(14–15). In fashion terms, Benedick says that his military friend's admiration of 'good armour' (16) has now given way to the vanity of a self-conscious young man who wishes to impress in civilian clothes ('a new doublet', 17). Lastly, Benedick claims that Claudio's very language has changed from the 'plain' (18) and straight-forward speech of 'an honest man' (19) to a 'fantastical banquet' of words (20). It is difficult to judge whether or not Benedick is fair in his observations, given that we only see Claudio after his return from the wars. Nonetheless, Benedick's own cynicism about love contrasts with Claudio's enthusiastic but inexperienced approach to relationships.

Victim or violator?

In Act III scene 2, Claudio hears Don John's accusations against Hero. Claudio's reaction to these allegations provides perhaps the strongest evidence of his weaknesses as a character. Even before Don John levels his accusation against Hero, he recognises that his case looks weak, protesting to Claudio 'You may think I love you not' (85). In these circumstances, it is worrying that Claudio is so willing to credit Don John's lies. There is a stark contrast between Don Pedro's scepticism ('I will not think it', 107) and Claudio's readiness to believe ('May this be so?', 107). This is compounded by the fact that Claudio swiftly devises a plan for the maximum humiliation of Hero ('where I should wed, there will I shame her', 112–13). It is left to Don John to remind the two noblemen that evidence of her infidelity is required, as he claims he will 'let the issue show itself' (117–18). Nonetheless, we are given the impression that Borachio's hoax will only confirm Claudio's pessimistic view of his fiancée.

Despite this setback to their relationship, it is crucial to a traditional comic interpretation of the play that we see Claudio and Hero happily reunited. However, if we feel Claudio's repentance is insincere, it is difficult to imagine that he will prove a deserving husband for Hero. As soon as Borachio's evidence confirms that Claudio's betrothed was wrongly accused, Claudio begs Leonato for forgiveness: 'Impose me to what penance your invention / Can lay upon my sin' (V.1.260–61). By admitting his fault and agreeing to restore Hero's reputation publicly (reading her **elegy** at the family monument in Act V scene 3), Claudio makes a reconcilia-tion between them possible. Nonetheless, Antonio's final judgement, 'I am glad that all things sort so well' (V.4.7) is perhaps a little premature. Even as he admits his guilt, Claudio tries to mitigate his actions by declaring 'yet sinned I not / But in mistaking' (V.1.261–62). Although he weeps for his wrongs (280), a modern audience is left with a nagging sense that any self-respecting woman would not take back a man who had behaved as Claudio has done. In the 2005 BBC production of the play, which uses an almost entirely rewritten script, Billie Piper as Hero declares that she would not get back together with her would-be husband 'in a million years'; a choice which would not have been afforded any actress playing Hero in the sixteenth century.

Dogberry and the Watch

The watchmen who appear in so many of Shakespeare's plays are quite different from the police officers we know today. In Elizabethan times, such law enforcers were paid by individual citizens according to the service they did, and they were virtually powerless to apprehend people of a higher social rank. Under such circumstances, their powers were severely limited, and the caricature of the incompetent watchman therefore became a rich source of comedy for Shakespeare and his contemporaries.

Dogberry and his watchmen make their first appearance in Act III scene 3 and only appear subsequently in Act III scene 5 and Act IV scene 2. They rarely have contact with Messina's noble classes, and recede into the background as the play concludes. Nonetheless, they have an immediate and significant effect on the plot and tone of the play. Their blundering is a great source of humour, and the plot could not be resolved without their involvement.

In plot terms, the intervention of the Watch (who overhears Borachio telling Conrade of his successful plan to disgrace Hero) is the catalyst that brings about the play's 'happy' ending. Without it, the tragic course of events might not be replaced with a sense of justice, mass reconciliation and harmony.

On a comic level, much amusement can be gleaned from the two watchmen's inability to follow the thread of Borachio and Conrade's conversation in Act III scene 3. Borachio quips about the changeable nature of fashion, asking Conrade 'seest thou not what a deformed thief this fashion is?' (121), much to the confusion of the First Watchman. Lost in wordplay and **metaphor**, he concludes that 'Deformed' is the name of a person, indeed a 'vile thief' (123). He continues this misunderstanding, declaring after the arrest of Conrade and Borachio that 'Deformed is one of them' (163). The Second Watchman then chimes in, threatening 'You'll be made bring Deformed forth, I warrant you' (166–67).

The overall dramatic role of Dogberry and his Watch is quite complex, blending comic incompetence with the disturbing possibility that the play could end in tragedy. We may laugh at Dogberry's feeble instructions to his men that they should send drunks to bed unless they refuse (III.3.41–47), and apprehend thieves without touching them (in case they should be 'defiled' by doing so, 56), but the consequence of this light-hearted bumbling could, in the eyes of the audience, be the death and disgrace of the innocent Hero. The Watch therefore serves the important plot function of setting the wheels of justice in — painfully slow — motion, whilst simultaneously building tension, as we wonder whether their amusing ineptitude will end in disaster.

Legal speak

Dogberry's control of language is charmingly loose, resulting in an array of amusing jokes and **puns**, particularly in Act III scene 3. He uses the word 'desartless' (III.3.9) in place of 'deserving', replaces 'sensible' (22) with 'senseless', and tells his men to 'comprehend' (24) rather than 'apprehend' any lawbreakers. Dogberry's language

even spreads to his watchmen, who 'recover' (161) rather than 'discover' Borachio's treason, and term it 'lechery' rather than 'treachery' (162). Sometimes the incorrect words are actually quite apt, as they point to underlying truths or themes in the main plot. This can produce **dramatic irony**, as when Dogberry asks in the opening line of Act IV scene 2, 'Is our whole dissembly appeared?' Although he means to say 'assembly', the word 'dissemble', meaning deceive or falsify, is more fitting for the deceitful Borachio.

Part of the reason for Dogberry's incessant use of malapropisms is that he is attempting to use the kind of elevated language that is associated with high social status. He agrees with the First Watchman that literacy is a good criterion for selecting a constable (III.3.9–12), and expresses the view that being able to read and write 'comes by nature' (15–16), as if it were inextricably connected to birth and rank. Like Margaret, who asks Benedick to write a sonnet for her in Act V scene 2, Dogberry sees language as a means of achieving social mobility or reflecting his refinement. This fallacy is exposed with brutal directness by Leonato in Act III scene 5, when he fails to understand Dogberry's absurdly inflated speech and states simply, 'Neighbours, you are tedious' (17). Leonato's brusque judgement underlines the class gap in the play, and creates tension as we wonder whether the ill-educated watchmen will be able to communicate Borachio's treachery to the noble classes before irrevocable damage is done.

Your local police farce

Unlike the police service we have today, Dogberry's Watch would not have had the powers to impose law and order on Messina without the goodwill of its citizens. The constable and his men only have jurisdiction over locals, as the officers are told to 'meddle with none but the Prince's subjects' (III.3.33–34). The watchmen have little power to control those who do not wish to comply with them, and Dogberry's command that they 'may stay' Don Pedro (i.e. arrest him, 74) if they see him during the night is qualified with the consideration that the prince must 'be willing' (78). This proviso illustrates the difficulty of policing a society with a strong class system. Conrade clearly thinks it is in his interests to call himself a 'gentleman' when he is arrested (IV.2.13), and officers were paid by those who benefited from their arrests (as we see when Leonato pays Dogberry, V.1.303). This system was obviously susceptible to corruption, the misuse of police powers and the collapse of the rule of law; thankfully Dogberry's chaotic force somehow achieves the restoration of order by the end of the play.

Courtship, music and dance

Much Ado About Nothing is one of Shakespeare's most musical plays, containing a wide variety of melodic interludes. These range from dances to serenades, sonnets

to **elegies**, and cover a wide range of human emotions. The song form is often associated with heightened feelings, as if regular **verse** or prose is less expressive of emotional range and depth. Even the title of the play hints at the thematic importance of music, since the word 'nothing' would have been pronounced to sound very much like 'noting' in Shakespeare's day, evoking the idea of musical notation. Wordplay along these lines is present in the exchange between Balthasar and Don Pedro in Act II scene 3 lines 52–55:

> BALTHASAR: Note this before my notes;
> There's not a note of mine that's worth the noting.
>
> DON PEDRO:
> Why, these very crotchets that he speaks;
> Note notes, forsooth, and nothing.

In Elizabethan times, people believed in the concept of the music of the spheres, where planets revolved as if in a dance, reflecting the harmony, or chaos, reigning in the heavens at any particular time. Such interstellar movements were believed to affect events on earth. Hence the emphasis on music in *Much Ado About Nothing* reflects the harmony or discord of relationships and events at different points in the play.

At the start of *Twelfth Night*, the lovesick duke Orsino listens to his musicians and proclaims 'If music be the food of love, play on', implying that music feeds a romantic atmosphere. In Act II scene 1 lines 64–71 of *Much Ado About Nothing*, Beatrice famously likens marriage to a dance:

> ...wooing, wedding, and repenting, is as a Scotch jig, a measure, and a cinquepace; the first is hot and hasty, like a Scotch jig, and full as fantastical; the wedding, mannerly-modest, as a measure, full of state and ancientry; and then comes repentance and, with his bad legs, falls into the cinquepace faster and faster, till he sinks into his grave.

This extended **metaphor** highlights the similarities between the conventions of **courtly love** and the prescribed steps of various dances. Beatrice advises Hero to be 'wooed in good time' (II.1.62), playing on the idea of rhythmic dancing whilst warning her not to rush into marriage. Taking the comparison further, she tells Hero that 'If the Prince be too important, tell him there is measure in everything and so dance out the answer' (62–64). Beatrice even applies the language of music to her own lovesickness in Act III scene 4, complaining that she is 'out of all other tune' (38). As a way of lifting her mistress's spirits, Margaret asks her to clap along to 'Light o'love' (39). Margaret also saucily claims that the song has no 'burden' (40), playing on the double meaning of the word as the refrain of a song or the weight of a man on top of a woman during intercourse (which Beatrice currently lacks, being single).

Having a ball

A ball was a major social event in Elizabethan times, and one of the best ways of meeting a romantic partner. As Nona Monahin notes **(www.hampshireshakespeare. org/notes/dance.html)**, hosting a ball was a way of displaying one's social status, and Leonato is clearly delighted to be entertaining Don Pedro and his companions in Messina. As in *Romeo and Juliet*, the ball itself acts as a catalyst for romance and intrigue between the various characters, and constitutes a **microcosm** of the rest of the play in the way it reflects interactions and dynamics. The characters' masks provide a perfect cover for teasing and sparring, as when Beatrice speaks disparagingly of Benedick to his face, pretending she does not know him (111–40). The anonymity granted by their disguises encourages all the characters to flirt more than usual, as we see in the exchanges between Beatrice and Don Pedro, Hero and Don Pedro, Margaret and Balthasar, and Antonio and Ursula. Although the theme of disguise is introduced in a comic form here, it also foreshadows the more sinister deceptions of Don John later in the play.

The thrust of *Much Ado About Nothing*'s plot derives from the masked ball in Act II scene 1, which provides a setting for romance (Claudio and Hero), deceit (Don John trying to trick Claudio), sexual tension and mistaken identity (Beatrice and Benedick). The dance at the end complements this opening scene, representing resolution and closure. In Elizabethan times, music was considered a symbol of divine and universal harmony, and those who attempted to disrupt its rhythms (in this case, Don John) threatened to destabilise this order. This too makes it fitting that the return to order at the end of the play should be celebrated in a rhythmic way, reflecting the harmony of the characters' relations to one another.

A courtly marriage

Like all Shakespearean comedies, the plot of *Much Ado About Nothing* revolves around the central characters' journeys towards marriage, and the related themes of love and sex. Even the play's title alludes to the courtship of women; in Renaissance English, 'nothing' was a slang term for female genitalia, in contrast to a man's 'thing'. With this in mind, the relaxed and sociable atmosphere of Messina provides the perfect backdrop for romance, for both Leonato's household and their noble visitors. Marriage rituals vary between societies and historical periods, and it is important to have an idea of Elizabethan courtship conventions in order to understand the world of *Much Ado About Nothing*.

Father's prerogative

In Shakespeare's time, women were considered domestic creatures who should depend on their fathers or husbands for financial support and the basic requirements

of food and shelter. It was therefore incumbent on a father to ensure that his daughter found a good husband, to whom he could pass on the rights and responsibilities of being her guardian. In return, a daughter would owe a debt of respect and obedience to her father, and would be expected to follow his wishes, even when offered an unappealing marriage. As we see in *Romeo and Juliet*, a woman could be disowned by her family if she were to object to a marriage arranged by her father. There are many 'missing' mothers in Shakespeare, and even those who are present, such as Lady Capulet, hold very little sway in deciding whether their daughters should accept or reject a suitor.

All for love?

Today, most people tend to think that love is the most important factor in deciding whom to marry. However, suitors in Shakespeare's day (particularly of the noble classes) were more concerned with a range of other factors, and this is reflected in the plays. Love was, of course, considered important, but many people believed that this affection could develop once a marriage had been agreed on a more sensible basis. Unlike today, most gentlewomen would marry at the age of about 14, as younger women were considered best for childbearing. Marriage between first cousins was also considered a good way of consolidating property and other business interests between close family members.

Money

Financial considerations were important for both men and women. A father would usually give away a dowry with his daughter in order to attract an eminent suitor, and some men would select a bride on this basis alone. Petruchio displays this attitude in Act I scene 2 of *The Taming of the Shrew*, when he claims 'I come to wive it wealthily in Padua; / If wealthily, then happily in Padua'. In the opening scenes of *The Merchant of Venice*, Portia's inherited wealth makes her an attractive prospect to suitors from all over the world. Financial concerns also play a role in *Much Ado About Nothing*, as we when Claudio enquires of Don Pedro in Act I scene 1, 'Hath Leonato any son, my lord?' (273). Don Pedro's negative reply makes Hero an even more attractive wife in Claudio's eyes, as she stands to inherit her father's wealth. Some critics use this line as evidence that Claudio is mercenary in his approach to marriage, but others regard his behaviour as merely typical of the times in which he lived. Even Beatrice notes in Act II scene 1 that it is important for a potential husband to have 'money enough in his purse' if he is to attract a wife (14).

Birth

Noble blood was also an important factor in match-making, as families tried to improve their social standing through alliances with others of a similar, or higher, rank. As governor of Messina, Leonato is clearly delighted at the prospect of Claudio (or indeed Don Pedro) marrying Hero, as both these men are of royal birth. Men of high rank could, however, find this a burden as well as a blessing. Beatrice exemplifies this fact when she responds to Don Pedro's teasing marriage proposal in Act II scene 1: 'No, my lord, unless I might have another for working-days: your grace is too costly to wear every day' (302–304).

Chastity

The main plot of *Much Ado About Nothing* hinges on the widespread view that female virginity and chastity were crucial to a successful marriage. The **patriarchal** society that encouraged this attitude did not expect men to be virgins on their wedding nights, and this double standard led to an obsession with women's sexual purity, as Claudio shows when he asks Don Pedro of Hero, 'Is she not a modest young lady?' (I.1.155). In contrast, women were expected to be sexually pure so that men could be sure that all the children produced in a marriage were their own. This helped fathers ensure that their property was passed on to a legitimate heir after they died. Such social attitudes were reinforced by religious beliefs of the time, which held that a woman's chastity was as important as her soul; a woman who had sex out of wedlock was therefore expected to go to hell.

Matchmaking

Given the convoluted system of courtship described above, matchmaking was a popular pursuit, though only men had the social freedom to take part in this pastime actively. This is exemplified in Don Pedro's intercession on Claudio's behalf to win Hero's hand, and the gulling of Beatrice and Benedick, which the Prince suggests. Indeed, Don Pedro asserts that 'we are the only love-gods' (II.1.357–58), clearly enjoying taking on Cupid's role. Some critics suggest that, as an older man, Don Pedro gets vicarious pleasure from helping others fall in love because he does not feel confident of winning himself a wife. Don John represents the **antithesis** of Don Pedro's good-natured desire to involve himself in others' wedding preparations, as he tries to destroy Hero and Claudio's relationship before it has begun.

As Beatrice and Benedick's relationship shows, even the least likely lovers could be persuaded to marry at a time when the pressure to adhere to social convention by finding a partner was much more powerful than it is today. Even as early as Act II scene 1, Beatrice watches Hero and Claudio's engagement and declares, 'Good Lord, for alliance! Thus goes every one to the world but I, and I am sunburnt; I may sit in a corner and cry "Heigh-ho for a husband!"' (293–95). Older unmarried women were often pitied as they had no means to support themselves independently, and women who had failed to produce children were likewise considered unfortunate or even abnormal. Indeed, when Benedick gives in to his love for Beatrice, he rationalises the change by reference to social pressure to produce an heir, arguing that 'the world must be peopled' (II.3.234–35).

Messina

Although Shakespeare almost certainly never visited Messina, he knew enough about European geography and politics to ensure that the setting of his play had an important bearing on its plot and characters.

Messina is a relatively small port city towards the northeast of the island of Sicily (see map). Although it may not have been a centre of politics, fashion or culture, it was nonetheless a fairly significant place. Its location on the Venetian sea route would have created important opportunities for foreign trade. At this time, Sicily was ruled by the Spanish, which explains why Leonato welcomes the Prince of Arragon (Don Pedro) so warmly. From Don Pedro's point of view, the city offers a tranquil retreat from military service where he can recuperate and find ready entertainment, and it is no surprise that he agrees to stay a month (I.1.140–41).

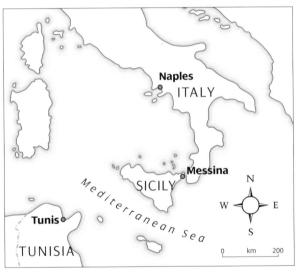

The island's gardens and leafy bowers provide the perfect cover for the benign romantic gullings of Don Pedro and his companions, as well as an overarching sense of fertility befitting a comedy. In dramatic terms, Shakespeare was able to draw on the 'foreignness' of his setting to evoke a sense of glamour and escapism. Setting the play abroad also enabled him to touch on contentious social issues that might have implied criticism of the state if he had located his tale in an English city.

Some directors have chosen to set the play in different locations (Kenneth Branagh memorably shot his 1993 film in lush Tuscan countryside), and the atmosphere of Messina is far more important than its geographical location. Richard Levin suggests in his chapter 'Crime and cover-up in Messina' in *Love and Society in Shakespearean Comedy* (1985) that it is the social **mores** of a small and tightly knit city that drive the plot of the play. In an atmosphere of upper-class conversation, rivalry, rumour and social manoeuvring, all is not quite as it seems, Levin argues: 'As soon as attention shifts from Don John's malevolence to the subtler social forces in Messina, everyone shares a measure of responsibility for all that happens' (p. 87). In this sense, the city is characterised far more by the behaviour of its citizens than by its outward appearance.

In recent years, some directors have returned to Shakespeare's original setting and have drawn on Sicily's more recent history as the island that produced the Italian

Mafia, an organisation that had its roots in close family ties and **patriarchal** pride. Although this historical development was obviously not on Shakespeare's mind when he chose to set *Much Ado About Nothing* in Messina, some directors have made good use of a modern Sicilian setting to reinterpret the play in relation to Mafiosa ideology.

Timing is everything

The time-scale chosen for any dramatic work has important consequences for the action, and Shakespeare's plays are no exception. His tragedies are often infused with a sense of time moving too quickly for sound judgements to be made, which can result in irrevocable disasters. This is certainly the case in *Othello*, where the **eponymous** hero wrongly murders Desdemona for committing adultery before she is given a chance to clear her name. In *The Winter's Tale*, however, we are shown the healing power of time, as the play includes a gap of 16 years at the beginning of Act IV. As these two examples show, the time scheme of a play has an important impact on the way we interpret it.

Without any significant cutting, *Much Ado About Nothing* might be expected to run for around four hours, including a brief interval.

The first reference to time is in Act I scene 1, when Don Pedro warns Benedick that he may come to regret his vocal opposition to marriage later in life. Using the old proverb 'In time the savage bull doth bear the yoke' (241), Don Pedro sets the scene for Benedick's comic change of attitude to women as the play goes on.

The swift tempo of the play's early scenes is emphasised in Act I scene 2, as Antonio reveals to Leonato his mistaken belief that Don Pedro intends to woo Hero, and, 'if he found her accordant, he meant to take the present time by the top and instantly break with you of it' (12–14). The sense of haste surrounding Hero's engagement (and the misunderstandings related to it) is ominous; in Shakespeare, events that happen too quickly are often the cause of regret. In Act II scene 3 of *Romeo and Juliet*, for example, Friar Laurence advises the young couple to proceed 'Wisely and slow' in their relationship, because 'they stumble that run fast'.

Beatrice highlights the importance of timing in courtship when she plays on the musical connotations of the word in Act II scene 1. Beatrice tells Hero that 'The fault will be in the music, cousin, if you be not wooed in good time. If the Prince be too important, tell him there is measure in everything and so dance out the answer' (61–64). Playing on the idea of 'time' as 'rhythm', Beatrice compares successful courting to a measured dance, in which the two participants are in step with one another.

Claudio is oblivious to Beatrice's advice regarding the importance of approaching marriage at a slow and steady pace. As soon as he is engaged to Hero, he displays his childlike impatience to get married, complaining that 'Time goes on crutches

till love have all his rites' (II.1.330–31). In contrast, Claudio's prospective father-in-law, Leonato, is glad of the delay, which will allow him to organise the wedding properly. He calls the following week 'a time too brief, too, to have all things answer my mind' (333–34). Don Pedro soothes Claudio's impatience by declaring that 'the time shall not go dully by us' (336–37) and devising the gulling of Beatrice and Benedick as a means of amusing the expectant wedding party.

After the leisurely slowing of time in the middle of the play, the action speeds up in Act III scene 4. Beatrice draws attention to the fact that last-minute preparations for the wedding are now taking place, telling Hero that "Tis almost five o'clock, cousin; 'tis time you were ready' (46–47). This reference to time serves to build tension and reminds us that potential disaster (in the form of Hero's disgrace at the altar) is rapidly approaching. This tension is exacerbated by Leonato's rushed exchange with Dogberry in Act III scene 5. The constable's verbose explanation forces the exasperated Leonato to beg him to be 'Brief, I pray you, for you see it is a busy time with me' (4–5). As Dogberry is incapable of this, Leonato leaves without learning of Borachio's plot.

Slow, slow, quick quick, slow

Claire McEachern points out in the Introduction to her Arden edition that *Much Ado About Nothing* is split into three distinct passages of time. The action of the play up to Act II scene 1 takes place over a day and an afternoon. Likewise, the period from Act IV scene 1 to the end of the play dramatises events very swiftly; no more than 24 hours elapse between Hero's disgrace and her reconciliation with Claudio in Act V scene 4. However, the central section of the play is longer. Having given his permission for Hero and Claudio to marry in Act II scene 1, Leonato explains in lines 332–33 that the ceremony will take place on 'Monday', which is 'hence a just seven-night' (i.e. a week later). The period of time between the beginning of Act II scene 2 and the start of Act IV is therefore a week long, affording time for the gulling of Benedick and Beatrice, and the execution of Don John's plan to disrupt Hero and Claudio's wedding.

One benefit of Shakespeare's uneven time scheme is that events can be dramatised at a pace that best suits their nature. The rapid courtship of Hero and Claudio is full of youthful impetuosity, but the slower pace of the middle of the play reflects the pleasant indolence of the noble classes amusing themselves whilst they await an important social event. The final third of the play has an increased tempo as tension shifts and the tone becomes darker. All this demonstrates the advantage of the irregular time scheme; the potentially tragic plot against Hero is infused with a sense of uncontrollable speed, whereas the more comic deception of Beatrice and Benedick is carried out at a leisurely pace. The gulling of Beatrice and Benedick certainly benefits from its slow unfolding, as an audience would find it difficult to believe that these two characters are capable of publicly swallowing their pride immediately after being tricked.

On a more philosophical level, Shakespeare exemplifies the theory that our perception of how quickly time passes is governed by what is happening to us. This idea lives on today in the phrase 'Time flies when you're having fun'. Indeed, Claudio's claim that 'Time goes on crutches till love have all his rites' (II.1.330–31) is reflected in the slower middle section of the play, while the credibility of the rash decisions and actions is increased by the sense that time is moving too quickly for fully formed judgements to be made.

A major disadvantage of breaking the **unity** of time is that it makes the play seem less **naturalistic**, and increases the difficulty audiences experience in **suspending their disbelief**. Time seems almost to stand still and then speed up again. This has important implications for the way we perceive Claudio's love for Hero, which seems to grow so quickly as to call its sincerity into question. It is possibly out of an awareness of this that Shakespeare inserts a reference to Claudio's previous affection for Hero ('I liked her ere I went to wars', I.1.284) and emphasises that he would have preferred a longer courtship; as he remarks to Don Pedro, 'lest my liking should too sudden seem, / I would have salved it with a longer treatise' (I.1.293–94). To some critics these insertions seem rather clumsy, and give the impression that Shakespeare is attempting to cover up the obvious difficulties of employing an uneven time scheme.

Love and war

The relationship between love and war goes back to classical times, when the two themes were linked through the character of the warrior-lover. Men like Homer's Odysseus and Virgil's Aeneas suffered as a result of having to choose between patriotic duty and physical desire. These two aspects of masculinity also frequently coincide and conflict in the Bible, as in the character of Samson. In the medieval period of chivalry, the courtly lover was a knight dedicated to a cause and devoted to his lady, whose favour he won through his military skills and dangerous quests, as well as by being handsome and attentive. In *Much Ado About Nothing*, as in so much literature, the themes of love and war reflect the eternal conflict between traditional 'masculine' values and the male pursuit of love.

Much Ado About Nothing is a romantic comedy set against the backdrop of a recent military conflict, so the themes of love and war are closely linked. Three of the main male characters are soldiers, and yet all are intricately involved in the courtship of Beatrice and Hero during the play. The two women are both objects of love, but are forced to overcome conflict before they can be happily married.

Love is…

Several different types of love are exemplified in the play, the first of which is Claudio's idealised love for Hero. Despite Claudio's claim that he 'liked her 'ere I went to wars' (I.1.284), we still get the impression that his feelings for Hero are fairly superficial. His attachment to her is strongly based on her beauty ('In mine eye she is the sweetest lady that ever I looked on', I.1.175–76) and the opinions of his companions. He is quick to ask Don Pedro 'Is she not a modest young lady?' (I.1.155), as if he is unsure of his own judgement in the matter. He is impressionable and idealistic in his view of love, and these traits lay the foundations for his deception by Don John later in the play.

Claudio, Benedick and Don Pedro's **homosocial** relationship also shows the power of love between close male friends. All three of the men are involved in the play's two courtships, and this infuses the romantic plots of the play with elements of male competition and humour. Benedick's love for Beatrice (and vice versa) seems to be based on a strong intellectual attraction, which we see in their verbal jousting. There are also hints that they previously had a relationship (II.1.253–58), which suggests that they know each other much better than Claudio and Hero. Although they are both initially averse to the idea of marriage, their pride is overcome by Don Pedro's plan, thereby effecting the change of opinion required for a comic 'happy' ending. Beatrice's steadfast loyalty to Hero shows the deep love she holds for her cousin and her indignation at the way women can be treated in a **patriarchal** society (an example of which occurs in Act II scene 1 lines 46–47, when Beatrice notes that 'it is my cousin's duty to make curtsy and say, "Father as it please you"').

Leonato's paternal love for Hero can be interpreted in a number of ways, not all of them positive. It could be argued that his desire to have his daughter well married impairs his judgement, since his decision to let Claudio marry her even after his disgraceful behaviour in Act IV suggests that he is willing to look beyond the best interests of his daughter in order to secure a favourable social connection. He is also happy for her to marry either Don Pedro or Claudio, which indicates that he is not particular about who his daughter marries, as long as he has an impressive lineage. However, Leonato's decision to challenge Claudio to a duel in Act V scene 1 suggests that his love for Hero ultimately overrides his selfishness, as he is willing to risk his life for her honour.

Finally, Margaret's love for Borachio causes her to take part in the plot against Hero and Claudio. Her behaviour shows the perils of misguided love, and the way that love can be used to manipulate others.

All's fair in love and war

In Elizabethan times, a soldier would have had a very close relationship with his male military comrades. This often fostered a 'boys' club' atmosphere, in which women were talked of disparagingly, and male friendships were trusted before women.

Military **machismo** and **courtly love** were therefore not easily compatible, as Claudio explains to Don Pedro in lines 276–79 of Act I scene 1:

> When you went onward on this ended action,
> I looked upon her [Hero] with a soldier's eye,
> That liked, but had a rougher task in hand
> Than to drive liking to the name of love;

It is only now that he is back from the battlefield that Claudio feels able to devote himself to wooing Hero properly. We see this tendency in *Othello*, where the **eponymous** hero's career as a general has left him little time to move in courtly circles, and he is therefore inexperienced in love. The villain Iago plays on this insecurity, using Othello's trust of his fellow soldier as a way of destroying him and his newly wedded wife.

Much Ado About Nothing is infused with an atmosphere of male honour that is bound up with ideas of swift military justice and mutual male trust. Don John's perfidy highlights the dangers of basing important judgement on this value system; Claudio and Don Pedro could both be accused of judging Hero too quickly and administering summary 'justice' without properly checking the facts of the case.

Themes

The themes of *Much Ado About Nothing* tend to relate both to the play's lighter, comic aspects and its darker, more sinister undertones. In this sense, the play is about opposites; love and hate, loyalty and deceit, and so on. Many of the themes are built into the structure of the play, so that, for instance, the inclusion of the masked ball scene illustrates that theatre is itself an illusion, with every actor playing a role.

When the themes of the play are considered together, Shakespeare seems to be preoccupied with issues of order. He explores the social hierarchies of class and gender, systems of political power, and the 'natural' order that depends on family ties and bonds of loyalty and love. The capacity of malevolence to destabilise these orders is demonstrated but does not ultimately prevail.

Conflict/war

The play begins at the end of a military action between Don Pedro and Don John's forces, and this provides a fitting backdrop for a plot which revolves around conflicts between individuals and groups. Seemingly intent on sparking a gender conflict, Beatrice holds her chauvinistic male companions to account for their views about women, whilst her linguistic battle with Benedick belies their underlying affection for one another. In this sense, both of these characters experience an internal conflict between pride and the desire to marry. Don John's group represents the evil elements in society, who are in constant conflict with the ruling classes and seek to destabilise them through their malicious behaviour.

Mistaken identity and disguise

Errors in identifying people, and the use of disguise, are rife throughout the play, from the masked ball scene through to Margaret's impersonation of Hero at her window. On several occasions during the ball scene we see characters lie about their identity, or deliberately pretend not to know the people they are addressing. This results in **dramatic irony**, or a sense of a gap between what we as the audience see and what the different characters are aware of. This can generate humour (as in Beatrice's mischievous teasing of Benedick in Act II scene 1) or tension (as when Margaret's impersonation of Hero is successful). All these cases of confusion contribute to the central comic theme of identity, with each character learning something new about who they are by the end of the play.

Deceit

Deception pervades every aspect of the play, though it is not always used malevolently. Don John's plot illustrates the harm that can be done by maliciously deceitful behaviour, but Don Pedro's plan to trick Beatrice and Benedick into loving one another exemplifies the benign comic potential of the 'white lie'. The word 'deceit' is also closely linked to the idea of illusion. In Act V scene 1, Borachio admits that 'I have deceived even your very eyes' (220–21) by talking to Margaret at Hero's window, revealing how he misled Claudio and his friends through the evidence of their own senses. In doing so, he reminds us that even the play we are watching is an artificial construct, an elaborate and entertaining illusion. Ironically in a play in which the male characters seem obsessed with female fidelity, Balthasar's song in Act II scene 3 states that 'Men were deceivers ever' (61), alerting us to the potential for hypocrisy in matters of love.

Families and bonds

Love is a central theme in all of Shakespeare's comedies, and it comes in many different forms in *Much Ado About Nothing*. Claudio's **courtly love** for Hero is tinged with a lack of understanding or trust, which causes him to become jealous. Leonato's paternal love for Hero is overridden by self-love and a distorted sense of honour. Both these characters show how the powerful emotion of love can turn to hate. In contrast, Beatrice and Benedick exemplify the way that apparent antipathy or enmity can change to love. In the end, the purest or most 'natural' forms of love prevail: families are reunited, two engagements take place, and the malevolent characters are punished for their destructive impulses.

The notion of family is closely related to ideas of 'nature' and behaving 'naturally', since people feel strong ties to their blood relations. Don John's hatred for his brother Don Pedro is a manifestation of his 'unnatural' or bastard birth, whereas Hero's obedience to her father shows her natural goodness. The family is also a means of control, as we see in Leonato's contrasting attitudes towards Hero

and Beatrice. As his niece, Beatrice is given far more freedom than his daughter Hero, whose behaviour he monitors closely. This is crucial, given that family ties also influence political connections. Hero's marriage to Claudio is advantageous because it brings together Messina's ruling classes with those of Florence, thus giving Leonato increased political influence and ensuring peace and prosperity in the future.

Honour and loyalty

These qualities are both highly valued by the men of the play, and govern every aspect of their behaviour. However, their social code seemingly does not extend to their treatment of Messina's women. By refusing to trust Hero's honesty in Act IV scene 1, Claudio, Leonato and Don Pedro all claim to be defending one another's honour, but they are ready to disgrace a daughter, fiancée and friend without even listening to her defence. Don Pedro claims that he stands 'dishonoured' for having tried 'To link my dear friend to a common stale' (IV.1.62–63), and in this he shows the destructiveness of injured male pride. In stark contrast, Benedick responds to the crisis by showing his loyalty to Beatrice and her cousin.

Music and dance

The musical elements of *Much Ado About Nothing* are entertaining, but they also have serious thematic implications. In many ways, music and dance provide a central **metaphor** for the play. For example, in the masked ball in Act II scene 1 we see the possibility of the harmonious state of Messina being disrupted by confusion and intrigue, whereas the dance at the end of the play signals a return to harmony after the discord caused by Don John and his followers. The songs and references to music in between all relate to the central theme of love and its trials and tribulations.

Miscommunication

The scenes featuring Dogberry and his inept watchmen show the problems caused by miscommunication. By repeatedly misunderstanding crucial information, and misusing language, these men jeopardise the course of justice. Dogberry's verbosity in Act III scene 5 even causes Leonato to leave for his daughter's wedding without sitting in on the examination of Borachio and Conrade. Rumour and eavesdropping also have crucial functions in the play, as we see in the two gulling scenes, and the gossip surrounding Don Pedro's attempts to woo Hero on Claudio's behalf. Of course, a great deal of the play's humour also derives from Beatrice and Benedick's inability to express the love they feel for one another.

Repentance and forgiveness

These go hand in hand, as the former precedes the latter. *Much Ado About Nothing* is one of Shakespeare's comedies, and one of the conventions of the **genre** is that the action ends in resolution and the restoration of peace and normality. Don John's

plan threatens to destabilise Messinian society, but in the end order prevails. Although he faces punishment for his actions, Claudio and Don Pedro are forgiven for their misjudgement, and even Margaret is shown leniency for her part in the plot against Hero. This sense of reconciliation suggests a more stable future for everyone, unlike the popular genre of revenge tragedies, which invariably ended up with a stage full of dead bodies because each act of vengeance spawned another.

Class and rank

Much Ado About Nothing features characters from a number of different backgrounds, and the interplay between them is crucial to the play's outcome. Margaret's tendency to fantasise about social mobility, for example, may well explain her willingness to impersonate Hero. Borachio's behaviour is largely motivated by the receipt of money from his wealthy companion Don John. Dogberry's desire to use sophisticated language indicates that he too is a social climber, although his tendency to speak nonsense almost leads to disaster by preventing the exposure of Don John's plot in time to prevent Hero's wedding-day humiliation. In all of these cases, the transfer of information, money and favours between different social classes has a direct influence on the plot, before social order is finally restored to Messina.

Images

Imagery is figurative language, using **similes** or **metaphors**, which fires the imagination by presenting pictures to the brain in a memorable way. Shakespeare's imagery repays close study, as each play has its own recurring images in addition to the typical and traditional images of the Elizabethan period, such as those pertaining to madness and reason, light and dark, bonds and divisions. The language of the comedies is dominated by images of love and the heart, and the images chosen by each character in *Much Ado About Nothing* are particularly important in conveying their respective attitudes to the play's central theme. For some, love is a game or a sport; for others it is as serious as war or a disease that requires a cure. In addition to reinforcing themes, imagery lends each text atmosphere and progression.

Taken all together, the imagery explores the different views of love that are expressed during the course of the play. Some of the language emphasises the harmony between men and women, while some depicts gender relations as continuous conflict. Through the sheer richness of the figurative language he uses, Shakespeare is thus able to explore the social rite of the courting game from a wide range of perspectives.

Hunting and fishing

Hunting and fishing have long been used as a **metaphor** for the pursuit of love, with a male usually perceived as 'hunting' for a female partner. Fishing in particular was

associated with trickery or deception in love, as fish are lured on to a rod by means of bait. It is therefore appropriate that in Act II scene 3, Claudio comments during the gulling of Benedick that he and his companions must 'Bait the hook well; this fish will bite' (110–11). In the parallel gulling scene where Hero and her maids deceive Beatrice, such language is even more prevalent. Ursula (III.1.26–29) declares that:

> The pleasant'st angling is to see the fish
> Cut with her golden oars the silver stream,
> And greedily devour the treacherous bait;
> So angle we for Beatrice

The imagery of trapping animals is once again apparent in Ursula's assertion that Beatrice has been 'limed' (i.e. caught like a bird in a sticky substance, III.1.104) by their cunning ploy, and Hero agrees that 'Some Cupid kills with arrows, some with traps' (III.1.106).

Sight and illusion

The language of sight and illusion is particularly noticeable in Act IV scene 1, when Hero's alleged licentiousness conflicts with her modest demeanour. In his anger, Claudio exclaims to his betrothed, 'Out on thee! Seeming!' (54), suggesting that her apparent infidelity is made worse by her innocent appearance. He says, 'You seem to me as Dian [the goddess of chastity] in her orb' (55), but claims that she is in fact 'intemperate in [her] blood' (57). Her lovely exterior had led him to believe that she possessed inner beauty too, and his disillusionment in this is expressed in lines 98–100: 'What a Hero hadst thou been, / If half thy outward graces had been placed / About thy thoughts and counsels of thy heart!' Having been made to 'see' Hero's infidelity by Don John, Claudio becomes obsessed with the idea that he cannot trust his own senses, asking 'Are our eyes our own?' (IV.1.69).

Don Pedro is also angered by what he believes to be Hero's deceptive appearance, and he employs imagery of sight and illusion when he commands Leonato, 'Give not this rotten orange to your friend; / She's but the sign and semblance of her honour' (IV.1.30–31). It is only after Borachio admits his villainy in Act V scene 1 that Hero's appearance is once again recognised as a true reflection of her character, as Claudio acknowledges when he declares, 'Sweet Hero, now thy image doth appear / In the rare semblance that I loved it first' (238–39).

Money and wealth

Throughout the play, the language of finance is used to define the relationships between different characters. When Claudio reveals his interest in Hero in Act I scene 1, Benedick teases him, enquiring, 'Would you buy her, that you inquire after her?' (168). Claudio's response, 'Can the world buy such a jewel?' (169), suggests that the women of Messina are perceived as a commodity to be bought, and that

Hero's beauty makes her priceless. In a similar way, Borachio is aware in Act III scene 3 that his arrest is likely to bring a financial reward to the watchmen, declaring that he and Conrade 'are like to prove a goodly commodity' (171).

Horns and cuckoldry

All the characters in the play are aware of the danger, and humour, associated with the cuckold's horns. Claudio jokes that Benedick would be 'horn-mad' if he were ever to marry, fuelling his friend's fear of women's infidelity (see, for example, I.1.242–47). As Benedick prepares to swallow his pride and publicly admit his feelings for Beatrice, Claudio teases him, declaring, 'we'll tip thy horns with gold' (44). Benedick's conversion in favour of marriage prompts him to recommend matrimony to Don Pedro, and the terms in which he now refers to the cuckold's horns reflect his change of heart: 'There is no staff more reverend than one tipped with horn' (V.4.121–22).

Beatrice compares the devil to 'an old cuckold with horns on his head' in Act II scene 1 (38), further illustrating how central the notion of sexual fidelity is to Messina's value system.

War and weaponry

The action of *Much Ado About Nothing* takes place following the military action between Don Pedro and Don John, and it is therefore no surprise that the language of war infuses the play. Claudio declares that before the war he looked at Hero 'with a soldier's eye' (I.1.277), suppressing his amorous impulses because of the prospective military campaign. Once back, he exchanges the language of war for the softer words of **courtly love**. In contrast, the exchanges between Benedick and Beatrice are characterised by far more aggressive vocabulary. Leonato notes that the two of them enjoy their 'merry war' (I.1.57), before asserting that 'they never meet but there's a skirmish of wit between them' (58–59). Benedick is wounded by Beatrice's words in Act II scene 1, complaining to Don Pedro that 'She speaks poniards, and every word stabs' (226–27). Having finally reached better terms with Beatrice, Benedick encounters another sharp wit in Margaret, who claims that his jibes against her are 'as blunt as the fencer's foils, which hit, but hurt not' (V.2.13–14). The idea of words as weapons is once again underlined in Benedick's response to Claudio's teasing: 'you break jests as braggarts do their blades, which, God be thanked, hurt not' (V.1.179–81).

Religion

In her moment of disgrace in Act IV scene 1, Hero exclaims 'O God defend me!' (75), exemplifying her piety even as others call it into question. The way each character speaks about God tells us a great deal about them and their moral code. Both Beatrice and Benedick use religious language to explain their aversion to

marriage. While Beatrice puts forward the general objection that 'Adam's sons are my brethren, and, truly, I hold it a sin to match in my kindred' (II.1.56–57), Benedick avows a particular distaste for Beatrice: 'I would not marry her, though she were endowed with all that Adam had left him before he transgressed' (II.1.229–31). The similarity of the imagery they use is an unwitting indication of how well suited they are to one another, even as they profess the opposite. It is fitting that their eventual union is celebrated as 'A miracle!' by Benedick himself in Act V scene 4 line 91.

The seasons

The seasons, which represent natural change, fertility, youth or warmth of emotion, are often invoked as a means of exploring the relationships between, or attitudes of, characters in the play. Beatrice proclaims she will not love Benedick until a 'hot January' (I.1.87), implying that it will never happen. In Act I scene 3, Don John describes Hero as a 'March-chick' (52) — in other words a woman who, like a bird born in spring, is precocious in contemplating marriage so young. Likewise, Leonato refers to Claudio's 'May of youth' (V.1.76) when challenging him to a duel, implying that he is young and full of life. Earlier in the play, Conrade uses seasonal imagery when he advises Don John to execute his plan for deceiving his brother at the optimum time, noting that 'it is needful that you frame the season for your own (I.3.23–24). Finally, Don Pedro notes Benedick's discomfort at his friends' teasing in Act V scene 4, asking why he is frosty and unpleasant, with 'such a February face' (V.4.41).

Clothing and fashion

Beatrice claims that Benedick is changeable in his loyalties, casting off his friends as he would old fashions: 'he wears his faith but as the fashion of his hat' (I.1.69–70). In Act III scene 3, Borachio and Conrade pick up the fashion analogy, suggesting that 'the fashion wears out more apparel than the man' (135–36); in other words, fashion is a symbol of fickleness or inconstancy, and has a tendency to make people look stupid. This is precisely what Beatrice fears if she again entrusts her heart to Benedick. In Act III scene 4 Margaret draws a comparison between the duchess of Milan's wedding gown, with its 'cloth o' gold, and cuts, and laced with silver, set with pearls, down-sleeves, side-sleeves, and skirts, round underborne with a bluish tinsel' (III.4.18–20), and Hero's simpler one. Ornamented with her own purity, chastity and humility, Hero's dress 'is worth ten on't' (21).

Food

Food is associated with the deadly sin of gluttony and other forms of excessive behaviour. Beatrice first refers to Benedick as 'stuffed' in Act I scene 1 (52), suggesting that he is full of pride. Whereas the Messenger suggests that Benedick

is a brave man, 'stuffed with all honourable virtues' (52–53), Beatrice concedes only that he is greedy, with 'an excellent stomach' (I.1.47–48). Later Benedick explains his change of heart regarding Beatrice by saying that 'A man loves the meat in his youth that he cannot endure in his age' (II.3.231–32) — in other words, a man's opinion of love, like his taste in food, may change as he gets older.

Illness and disease

In Shakespeare's time, love was often described as an illness that affected the body and the mind. When Don Pedro agrees to woo Hero for Claudio, there is imagery of illness and medical treatment in Claudio's thanks: 'How sweetly you do minister to love' (I.1.291). Claudio hopes his love will be 'salved' (294) by Don Pedro's action, and Don Pedro promises his friend 'a remedy' in the shape of Hero's hand in marriage (298). Benedick claims, 'I have the toothache', when he is in fact sighing for love of Beatrice (III.2.20), whilst Beatrice exclaims, 'By my troth, I am exceeding ill' (III.4.47). When Beatrice complains of a stuffy cold, Margaret teasingly offers her some 'Carduus Benedictus' to clear her nose (III.4.66–67), implying that the man who has made Beatrice lovesick could also supply the cure. Even when the pair are finally united, imagery of lovesickness remains central to their conversation. Benedick says his friends 'swore you were almost sick for me', and Beatrice replies that hers 'swore that you were well-nigh dead for me' (V.4.80–81). Teasingly pretending she loves him out of pity, Beatrice claims she will love Benedick 'partly to save your life, for I was told you were in a consumption' (V.4.95–96).

Music

The language of music and the idea of harmony are closely linked to the play's various love affairs and their outcomes. Balthasar suggests that love and music are virtually synonymous with one another, declaring in Act II scene 3 that 'Because you talk of wooing, I will sing' (47). In a cynical speech to Hero in Act II scene 1, Beatrice uses imagery of music and dance to warn Hero that while people fall in love quickly, they may spend a much longer time regretting their marriage: 'For hear me, Hero: wooing, wedding, and repenting, is as a Scotch jig, a measure and a cinquepace' (64–66). When Beatrice is lovesick for Benedick, Hero asks her, 'Do you speak in the sick tune?', and she declares, 'I am out of all other tune, methinks' (III.4.37–38).

Animals

In Act I scene 1, Beatrice and Benedick exchange a series of animal-related insults. Benedick calls Beatrice a 'parrot-teacher' (130), suggesting that she talks gibberish, and she retorts, 'A bird of my tongue is better than a beast of yours' (131–32). He then declares, 'I would my horse had the speed of your tongue, and so good a continuer' (133–34). Don Pedro uses an animal **metaphor** to predict that Benedick

will eventually submit to matrimony: 'In time the savage bull doth bear the yoke' (I.1.241). All of these references show that the Elizabethans were conscious of their superiority to animals in the chain of being, and used comparisons with animals to tease or insult one another.

Seeing and believing

The relationship between appearance and reality is a recurring theme in Shakespeare's plays. Theatre is the art of making audiences believe what they see, of evoking, as Coleridge put it, 'a willing **suspension of disbelief**'. We must feel that the characters are thinking and feeling what they are pretending to, that the people, places and events of the play are real. Shakespeare had to achieve this without scenery and using boy actors for women's parts. In *Much Ado About Nothing*, paradoxically, the reality behind appearances is itself unstable. Nearly every scene of the play depends upon or refers to constructions or misconstructions of something that has been seen or heard, and it falls to the audience to try to interpret things correctly.

Many Elizabethans believed that external appearance revealed inner truth, but Shakespeare was interested in exploring the problem of a fair exterior that belies an inner foulness. His plays explore the issues of seeing, seeming and dissembling, and, particularly in the comedies, disguise and deception are recurring themes. The seventeenth-century French philosopher René Descartes asked what grounds we have for believing we can trust the evidence of our perceptions, since in dreams we believe to be true that which in waking proves to be delusory, and therefore our normal waking life may also turn out to be a dream. In the twentieth century, Ludwig Wittgenstein pointed out that real truth does not look any different from apparent truth, and therefore we cannot trust the evidence of our eyes: the sun circling the earth would look the same to us as the earth circling the sun.

Do my eyes deceive me?

Much Ado About Nothing is full of references to eyes and vision. Beatrice's asssertion in Act II scene 1 that 'I have a good eye, uncle' (II.1.73–74) immediately links the action of seeing to the issues of judgement and attitude. Soon after this, Claudio's sudden love for Hero causes Benedick to ask in his **soliloquy**, 'May I be so converted and see with these eyes?' (II.3.21–22), suggesting that falling in love is a matter of looking at life in a certain way. This is underlined by Margaret's teasing of Beatrice in Act III scene 4, when she declares 'methinks you look with your eyes as other women do' (82–83). In other words, Beatrice's seeming affection for Benedick has changed the way she looks at the world.

The theme of illusion is also closely linked to the concept of perspective. Hero's disgrace is entirely imaginary, and is dependent on the play's male characters believing the evidence of their eyes. Leonato is so shocked by Claudio's accusations

that he asks, 'Are these things spoken, or do I but dream?' (IV.1.64), while Claudio retorts by asking a series of rhetorical questions (IV.1.67–69):

> Leonato, stand I here?
> Is this the Prince? Is this the Prince's brother?
> Is this face Hero's? Are our eyes our own?

Unfortunately, the answer to the last question is, in **metaphorical** terms, a resounding 'no': as Borachio confesses to the assembled noblemen in Act V scene 1, he has 'deceived even your very eyes' (221). His comment reminds us that villains in Shakespeare, like Iago or Edmund, often succeed in their aims by persuading credulous characters to see events from their own twisted point of view.

A matter of perspective

As in real life, all the characters in the play are inclined to see events in a way that is consistent with their view of the world; Benedick, for example, sees Beatrice as a 'curst' woman largely because he has a negative view of women in general. In Claudio's case, the reports of Hero's infidelity fulfil his worst fears, and he expresses his feelings of emotional hurt as anger, much like Leontes in *The Winter's Tale*. Claudio does not know Hero well enough to trust her, and he has spent so long in the company of the sworn **misogynist** Benedick that he is disconcertingly ready to believe the worst of his fiancée.

This illustrates an important **dichotomy** in *Much Ado About Nothing* between characters who try to find 'proof' of others' faults and those who show faith in others' goodness. Claudio and Don Pedro (and, initially, Leonato) fall into the category of doubters, who rely on masculine ideas of honesty and truth, which let them down. Claudio is twice described as having been 'possessed' by Don John's deceitful words (III.3.145 and 150), and this impairs his judgement. Leonato is also bound by a naïve and snobbish view that men of high birth would never deceive him ('Would the two Princes lie, and Claudio lie[?]', IV.1.150) and therefore disowns his daughter without looking into the facts of her case.

In stark contrast, Benedick diverges from the view of his male companions, and instead trusts in Beatrice's conviction that Hero is honest. Beatrice's belief has no evidence to back it up; like the Friar, who wagers his 'divinity' on Hero's innocence (IV.1.166), she simply has faith in her cousin. Ultimately, this confidence is justified by Borachio, who points out to Claudio and his companions that his treachery would not have been so successful if they had been less willing to believe Don John's lies: 'what your wisdoms could not discover, these shallow fools [Dogberry and his men] have brought to light' (V.1.221–23).

Ultimately, characters' opinions depend on the things they see and hear, as well as the way they react to all these circumstances. The only people lucky enough to enjoy **omniscience** are the audience, since we witness deceptions, private conversations

and dramatic ironies about which the other characters are ignorant. By structuring *Much Ado About Nothing* in this way, Shakespeare reminds us not only that theatre is an illusion, made up of a variety of different perspectives, but that our own lives are determined by our own very limited views of the world around us.

Quotations

The best quotations to learn are those that you have found useful in class discussions and practice essays, and they will require little conscious learning because you are already familiar with them. The most effective ones to learn in addition are those that serve more than one purpose, i.e. that can be used to support a theme or image usage as well as a point about character or dramatic effect. Consider what sort of ideas you could support with each quotation if you were writing an essay.

Act I scene 1

How much better is it to weep at joy than to joy at weeping! (*Leonato, ll. 26–27*)

There is a kind of merry war betwixt Signor Benedick and her... (*Leonato, ll. 56–57*)

Truly, the lady fathers herself. (*Don Pedro, ll. 102–103*)

...it is certain I am loved of all ladies, only you excepted... (*Benedick, ll. 116–17*)

...truly, I love none. (*Benedick, ll. 119*)

I had rather hear my dog bark at a crow than a man swear he loves me. (*Beatrice, ll. 123–4*)

...I will live a bachelor. (*Benedick, ll. 226–27*)

'In time the savage bull doth bear the yoke.' (*Don Pedro, ll. 241*)

...I liked her ere I went to wars. (*Claudio, ll. 284*)

And I will break with her and with her father
And thou shalt have her. (*Don Pedro, ll. 288–89*)

Act I scene 2

Hath the fellow any wit that told you this? (*Leonato, l. 15*)

...I will acquaint my daughter withal... (*Leonato, l. 19*)

Act I scene 3

I cannot hide what I am. (*Don John, ll. 12–13*)

...it is needful that you frame the season for your own harvest. (*Conrade, ll. 23–24*)

…I am a plain-dealing villain. (*Don John, ll. 29–30*)

…if I can cross him any way, I bless myself every way. (*Don John, ll. 62–63*)

Act II scene 1

By my troth, niece, thou wilt never get thee a husband if thou be so shrewd of thy tongue. (*Leonato, ll. 16–17*)

Well, niece, I trust you will be ruled by your father. (*Antonio, ll. 44–45*)

Yes, faith; it is my cousin's duty to make curtsy and say, 'Father, as it please you.' But yet for all that, cousin, let him be a handsome fellow, or else make another curtsy and say, 'Father, as it please me.' (*Beatrice, ll. 46–49*)

…I would he had boarded me. (*Beatrice, ll. 128–29*)

…the Prince woos for himself. (*Claudio, l. 159*)

Friendship is constant in all other things
Save in the office and affairs of love (*Claudio, ll. 160–61*)

I would not marry her, though she were endowed with all that Adam had left him before he transgressed. (*Benedick, ll. 229–31*)

…he won it of me with false dice… (*Beatrice, l. 257*)

…I was born to speak all mirth and no matter. (*Beatrice, ll. 304–05*)

…she mocks all her wooers out of suit. (*Leonato, ll. 323–24*)

Time goes on crutches till love have all his rites. (*Claudio, ll. 330–31*)

Act II scene 2

Any bar, any cross, any impediment will be medicinable to me…
(*Don John, ll. 5–6*)

…there shall appear such seeming truth of Hero's disloyalty that jealousy shall be called assurance, and all the preparation overthrown. (*Borachio, ll. 43–45*)

Act II scene 3

May I be so converted and see with these eyes? (*Balthasar, ll. 21–22*)

…till all graces be in one woman, one woman shall not come in my grace.
(*Benedick, ll. 27–28*)

Sigh no more, ladies, sigh no more,
Men were deceivers ever… (*Balthasar, ll. 60–61*)

Bait the hook well; this fish will bite. (*Claudio, ll. 110–11*)

…she says she will die, if he love her not; and she will die, ere she make her love known… (*Claudio, l. 173–75*)

Love me? Why, it must be requited. (*Benedick, ll. 218–19*)

…happy are they that hear their detractions and can put them to mending. (*Benedick, ll. 223–24*)

Act III scene 1

> Cupid's crafty arrow[…]
> […] only wounds by hearsay. (*Hero, ll. 22–23*)

> The pleasant'st angling is to see the fish
> Cut with her golden oars the silver stream,
> And greedily devour the treacherous bait;
> So angle we for Beatrice… (*Ursula, ll. 26–29*)

> But Nature never framed a woman's heart
> Of prouder stuff than that of Beatrice. (*Hero, ll. 49–50*)

> …I'll devise some honest slanders
> To stain my cousin with. (*Hero, ll. 84–85*)

Some Cupid kills with arrows, some with traps. (*Hero, l. 106*)

Contempt, farewell! and maiden pride, adieu! (*Beatrice, l. 109*)

…Benedick, love on; I will requite thee… (*Beatrice, l. 111*)

Act III scene 2

Gallants, I am not as I have been. (*Benedick, l. 14*)

Leonato's Hero, your Hero, every man's Hero. (*Don John, ll. 95–96*)

…where I should wed, there will I shame her. (*Claudio, ll. 112–13*)

Act III scene 3

We will rather sleep than talk; we know what belongs to a watch. (*First Watchman, ll. 37–38*)

…when rich villains have need of poor ones, poor ones may make what price they will. (*Borachio, ll. 110–12*)

I know that Deformed; 'a has been a vile thief this seven year… (*First Watchman, ll. 122–23*)

We have here recovered the most dangerous piece of lechery that ever was known in the commonwealth. (*Second Watchman, ll. 161–62*)

Act III scene 4

'Twill be heavier soon, by the weight of a man. (*Margaret, l. 24*)

…methinks you look with your eyes as other women do. (*Margaret, l. 82–83*)

Act III scene 5

...our watch, sir, have indeed comprehended two aspicious persons... (*Dogberry, ll. 42–43*)

Act IV scene 1

What men may do! What men daily do, not knowing what they do! (*Claudio, ll. 17–18*)

Give not this rotten orange to your friend;
She's but the sign and semblance of her honour. (*Claudio, ll. 30–31*)

Out on thee! Seeming! [...]
You seem to me as Dian in her orb,
As chaste as is the bud ere it be blown;
But you are more intemperate in your blood than Venus... (*Claudio, ll. 54–58*)

I stand dishonoured, that have gone about
To link my dear friend to a common stale. (*Don Pedro, ll. 63–64*)

Are our eyes our own? (*Claudio, l. 69*)

What kind of catechizing call you this? (*Hero, l. 76*)

...I'll lock up all the gates of love (*Claudio, l. 103*)

Death is the fairest cover for her shame... (*Leonato, l. 114*)

          ...O, she is fallen
Into a pit of ink, that the wide sea
Hath drops too few to wash her clean again... (*Leonato, ll. 137–39*)

O, on my soul, my cousin is belied! (*Beatrice, l. 144*)

...publish it that she is dead indeed. (*Friar, l. 202*)

She dying, as it must be so maintained,
Upon the instant that she was accused,
Shall be lamented, pitied, and excused... (*Friar, ll. 212–14*)

The supposition of the lady's death
Will quench the wonder of her infamy... (*Friar, ll. 236–37*)

Being that I flow in grief,
The smallest twine may lead me. (*Leonato, ll. 247–48*)

Kill Claudio. (*Beatrice, l. 285*)

O that I were a man for his sake, or that I had any friend would be a man for my sake! (*Beatrice, l. 312–13*)

...manhood is melted into curtsies... (*Beatrice, ll. 313–14*)

I cannot be a man with wishing, therefore I will die a woman with grieving. (*Beatrice, ll. 317–18*)

Act IV scene 2

O villain! Thou wilt be condemned into everlasting redemption for this. (*Dogberry, ll. 54–55*)

...remember that I am an ass... (*Dogberry, l. 74*)

Act V scene 1

...men
Can counsel and speak comfort to that grief
Which they themselves not feel; but, tasting it,
Their counsel turns to passion... (*Leonato, ll. 20–23*)

My soul doth tell me Hero is belied... (*Leonato, l. 42*)

...she was charged with nothing
But what was true and very full of proof. (*Don Pedro, ll. 104–105*)

You have killed a sweet lady, and her death shall fall heavy on you. (*Benedick, ll. 145–46*)

...I desire nothing but the reward of a villain. (*Borachio, ll. 231*)

...yet sinned I not
But in mistaking. (*Claudio, ll. 261–62*)

...since you could not be my son-in-law,
Be yet my nephew. (*Leonato, ll. 274–75*)

Act V scene 2

...I do suffer love indeed, for I love thee against my will. (*Benedick, ll. 61–62*)

Thou and I are too wise to woo peaceably. (*Benedick, l. 66*)

I will live in thy heart, die in thy lap and be buried in thy eyes... (*Benedick, ll. 92–93*)

Act V scene 3

So the life that died with shame
Lives in death with glorious fame. (*Claudio, ll. 7–8*)

Yearly will I do this rite. (*Claudio, l. 23*)

And Hymen now with luckier issue speed's
Than this for whom we rendered up this woe. (*Claudio, ll. 32–33*)

Act V scene 4

...I am glad that all things sort so well. (*Antonio, l. 7*)

Another Hero! (*Claudio, l. 62*)

She died, my lord, but whiles her slander lived. (*Leonato, ll. 66*)

...a college of wit-crackers cannot flout me out of my humour.
(*Benedick, ll. 99–100*)

...man is a giddy thing... (*Benedick, l. 106*)

Critical voices

The following review comments from the last three centuries show changing attitudes to the play and its characters. They offer useful support for your own opinion in a coursework or exam essay, and can provide evidence of opposing views. They also provide a basis for class discussion and offer new ways of looking at the text or the characters.

> ...this play we must call a comedy, tho' some of the incidents and discourses are more in a tragic strain. (Charles Gildon, 1710)

> ...he [Shakespeare] always draws men and women so perfectly that when we read we can scarce persuade ourselves but that the discourse is real and no fiction. (Charles Gildon, 1710)

> This fable [is] absurd and ridiculous [...] mangled and defaced, full of inconsistencies, contradictions and blunders. (Charlotte Lennox, 1753)

> This play is so witty, so playful, so abundant in strong writing, and rich humour, that it has always attracted universal applause. (Charles Dibdin, 1795)

> [The play is] one of Shakespeare's few essays at what may be called genteel comedy. (Samuel Taylor Coleridge, 1818)

> In Beatrice, high intellect and high animal spirits meet, and excite each other like fire and air. (Anna Brownell Jameson, 1832)

> ...his [Shakespeare's] most perfect comic masterpiece. For absolute power of composition, for faultless balance and blameless rectitude of design, there is unquestionably no creation of his hand that will bear comparison with *Much Ado About Nothing*. (Algernon Charles Swinburne, 1880)

> ...a superb play, bountiful in excitement, wit and beauty. (Joseph T. Shipley, 1956)

> Beatrice is the first woman in our literature, perhaps in the literature of Europe, who not only has a brain, but delights in the constant employment of it. (John Dover Wilson, 1962)

> ...Beatrice and Benedick display a kind of *agility* which is a condition of true life, and compared with them most other characters appear wooden and immobile. (Peter Hollindale, 1989)

> ...we might begin to think seriously about assigning *Much Ado About Nothing* to the category of 'problem plays'. (Graham Holderness, 1989)

> ...the people who triumph in it are those who speak in an idiom we all understand and can claim as our own. (Kenneth McLeish and Stephen Unwin, 1998)

Literary terms and concepts

The terms and concepts below have been selected for their relevance to talking and writing about *Much Ado About Nothing*. It will aid argument and expression to become familiar with them and to use them in your discussion and essays.

altruism acting unselfishly for the benefit of others.

ambiguity capacity of words to have two simultaneous meanings in the same context, either accidentally or, more often, as a deliberate device for enriching the meaning of text. For example, when Margaret talks of a 'burden' in Act III scene 4, she is alluding to the refrain of a song as well as the weight of a man on top of a woman (39–40).

ambivalence the simultaneous coexistence of opposing feelings or attitudes.

antithesis the exact opposite of something.

aside a remark spoken by a character in a play, which is shared with the audience but unheard by some or all of the other characters on stage. For example, Claudio speaks several asides in Act II scene 3, which Benedick cannot hear.

blank verse unrhymed **iambic pentameter**; the staple form of Shakespeare plays.

caesura a deliberate break in a line of poetry, signified by punctuation.

climax a moment of intensity to which a series of actions has been leading.

colloquial the informal language of speech rather than that of writing.

courtly love a formal system of love and courtship, governed by gender stereotypes and expectations.

crux (pl. cruces) a point for debate that is essential for resolving an argument.

cynic somebody who tends to expect the worst of human behaviour.

dénouement the unfolding of the final stages of a plot, when all is revealed; in French, it literally means 'untying'.

dichotomy a gulf or clear division between two things or ideas.

dramatic irony when the audience knows something the character speaking does not, which can create tension or humour and can therefore contribute to a tragic or comic mood. See, for example, the 'gulling' scenes, where Benedick and Beatrice believe they are secretly overhearing others' conversations about them.

elegy	a mournful song or poem composed to lament a death, as we see in Claudio's tribute to Hero.
enjamb(e)ment	a run-on instead of end-stopped line of poetry, usually to reflect or emphasise its meaning, e.g. 'And what have I to give you back, whose worth / May counterpoise this rich and precious gift?' (IV.1.25–26).
eponymous	where a name is also used as a title, e.g. Othello is the eponymous hero of Shakespeare's play *Othello*.
faux	an adjective used to describe an imitation of something, e.g. a faux leather handbag.
feminism	advocacy of women's rights and the equality of the sexes; in literary terms, a school of criticism concerned with analysing literature from a female perspective.
genre	a type or form of writing
harpy	a fearsome mythological creature that was half bird and half woman.
hermeneutics	the discipline of interpreting texts.
homosocial	describes those who tend to have friends of the same gender.
hyperbole	deliberate exaggeration for effect, e.g. 'I would not marry her, though she were endowed with all Adam had left him before he transgressed' (II.1.229–31).
iambic pentameter	a verse form using five metrical feet in each line, each foot comprising two syllables, the first of which is unstressed and the second of which is stressed.
in medias res	the technique of beginning a scene or chapter in the middle of an event or dialogue.
irony	a discrepancy between the actual and implied meaning of language; or an amusing or cruel reversal of an outcome expected, intended or deserved; a situation in which one is mocked by fate or the facts.
machismo	the exhibition of excessively male characteristics or behaviour.
malapropism	ridiculous misuse of a word, often because it sounds similar to one with a different meaning, e.g. Dogberry using 'comprehend' instead of 'apprehend' (III.3.24).

metaphor	a figure of speech in which one thing is described in terms of another, e.g. Claudio describes Hero as 'a jewel' (I.1.169).
micro/ macrocosm	a small/large thing that represents a larger/smaller thing. For example, Messina can be seen as a microcosm of Italy, whilst Italy is a macrocosm of Messina.
misogyny	a generalised hatred of women.
mores (pronounced 'mor-ays')	social conventions that govern the way people behave in a particular context.
motif	a recurring literary, verbal or structural device that develops or reminds the audience of a theme.
naturalism	a style of theatre that attempts to create the impression of reality on the stage.
nihilism	the belief that life is ultimately pointless and that human values are worth nothing.
objectification	when a person (usually a woman, in Shakespeare) is reduced to the status of an object, often as a means of controlling him/her.
omniscient	all-knowing; refers to a character or playwright's godlike knowledge.
patriarchy	a society in which men are dominant and privileged.
poetic justice	due allocation of reward and punishment for virtue and vice respectively.
post-structuralism	a school of criticism derived from structuralism, which analyses texts by questioning the basis upon which the structures of society's conventions and language have been established.
pun	use of a word with double meaning for humorous or ironic effect. For example, Margaret offers Beatrice a medicine called 'Carduus Benedictus' in Act III scene 4 (66–67), knowing that her illness is actually lovesickness for Benedick.
Puritans	a group of Protestants in sixteenth- and seventeenth-century England, who believed in strict moral and religious discipline, and simple acts of worship. They believed theatres encouraged debauchery and corruption, and Shakespeare and

his contemporaries therefore often had to tone down the content of their plays in order to avoid offending this powerful movement.

Renaissance   originating in Italy, the revival of art and literature under the influence of classical models in the fifteenth and sixteenth centuries in Western Europe.

rhetoric   persuasive language, which is carefully constructed to have a specific effect on the speaker's audience.

rhyming couplet   a pair of adjacent rhyming lines.

romance   a story of love and heroism, deriving from medieval court life and fairy tales.

simile   a comparison introduced by 'as' or 'like' ; e.g. Benedick tells Margaret 'Thy wit is as quick as the greyhound's mouth; it catches' (V.2.11–12).

soliloquy   a speech made by a character alone on stage, which reveals their thoughts.

sources   the stories or inspirations, drawn from history, mythology or other literary works, which writers build into their own artistic creation.

structuralism   a school of criticism that analyses texts according to the premise that human society is a network of interrelated elements that yield significant patterns.

suspension of disbelief   Coleridge used this expression to explain how an audience does not apply the normal rules of realism when watching drama but has a 'poetic faith' in theatrical conventions and accepts the illusion of the fictional world.

unities (the)   three principles of dramatic composition, deriving from Aristotle, whereby a play should consist of one related series of actions (unity of action), occur within one day (unity of time), and happen in one location (unity of place). Shakespeare observes the unities in *The Tempest* and in the second half of *Othello*.

verse   language organised according to its rhythmical qualities into regular patterns of metre and set out in lines.

Questions & Answers

LITERATURE

Essay questions, specimen plans and notes

Coursework essays

Below are some possible titles that would be appropriate for a coursework essay.

1 Explore how the language of the characters in *Much Ado About Nothing* reveals the social conventions and constraints of Shakespeare's time.

In answering a question like this you should:

- Define 'conventions' and 'constraints', and consider whether the two are synonymous.
- Give specific instances of different types of language (subservient, demanding, pitying), and explain what they show about the characters who speak them.
- Identify patterns of language, and whether they are organised along class, gender or other lines.
- Refer to key scenes in which such patterns are most clearly apparent.
- Explore the dramatic impact these scenes would have on the audience.
- Ascertain whether characters change the way they speak in certain situations (e.g. Hero) or over the course of the play (e.g. Beatrice, Benedick).
- Make reference to the differences between the structure of Shakespeare's society and our own, without making sweeping generalisations.
- Consider how a Shakespearean audience would have responded to the play, as compared to a modern one.
- Explore how language in the play is used for dramatic effect, the exposition of character and addressing the play's themes.
- Consider how the language of the play has been commented on by various critics.
- State your own view on how language reveals the social conventions and constraints of Shakespeare's time.

Examiners noted that excessively long coursework tended to lack focus. Weaker candidates often failed to attribute quotations (particularly from internet sources) and attempted to fulfil their obligations to AO5i by making sweeping historical generalisations, without necessarily answering the question set. Poor structure and proofreading were also a problem. Stronger candidates had a strong sense of the play's genre, and considered it as a dramatic text, referencing different productions and audience responses (AO2). For AO3, successful candidates not only quoted from the play, but provided insightful analysis of Shakespeare's language and discerning reference to critical opinions; once again, weaker candidates tended to substitute others' ideas for their own rather than analysing and questioning different critical perspectives.

(Source: Edexcel examiner's report, summer 2005)

Further questions

2 Explore how Shakespeare examines the themes of trust and jealousy in *Much Ado About Nothing*. Compare your interpretation of *Much Ado About Nothing* with that of other critics.

3 ANTONIO: Well, niece, I trust you will be ruled by your father.

BEATRICE: Yes, faith; it is my cousin's duty to make curtsy and say, 'Father, as it please you.' (II.1.44–47)

Does this exchange reflect Shakespeare's presentation of women in the play, and what is your response to this presentation 400 years later?

4 Consider the play's setting. How does Messinian society influence the tone of the play, and its outcomes?

5 Explore the character of Benedick, showing how he develops through the play and saying how convincing you find him.

6 Explore the character of Claudio, tracing and accounting for his behaviour throughout the play.

7 Choose any two characters who offer interesting points for comparison and contrast. Write a study of their roles in the play and your response to them as characters. (Suggestions: Hero and Beatrice; Don John and Don Pedro; Claudio and Benedick.)

8 Does Shakespeare succeed in individualising the minor characters? Consider four or five examples to support your answer.

9 Write about the use of imagery in *Much Ado About Nothing* and its contribution to the overall effect of the play.

10 What have you gained in your knowledge of Shakespeare and his period by your study of this play and its critics?

Exam essays

The exemplar essay questions that follow can be used for planning practice and/or full essay writing within the time limit, with or without the text. Many have been previously set by different exam boards for various specifications. In each of the three sections there are some essay titles with suggestions for ideas to include in a plan, and some with examiners' notes and guidance on how to approach the question.

Remember to write about the play and the audience, not the book and the reader, and try to visualise how it would appear on stage and how it would sound; the drama and the poetry are essential elements of the written text you are being asked to respond to. Here are the questions to address when analysing drama text passages:

- Is it all verse, all prose or a mixture?
- Is it primarily looking forward to something that is to come, or looking backwards to explain or reinforce a previous event?
- Are there any entrances or exits, and if so what effect do they have?

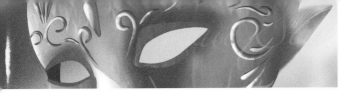

- Look at stage directions. What are the visual effects of the position of props and the actions being performed?
- Comment on the imagery and relate it to other usages and its link with themes.
- Is there a dominant or silent presence or one who is given relatively few lines?
- Is there any irony or dramatic irony? Who knows what at this stage?
- Where is the audience's sympathy, and why?
- How does this passage relate to other parts of the text? Is it similar to or a contrast to another episode?
- How do language and tone reveal character, and how do they affect the audience's feelings about something or someone?
- How does the scene add to plot and character, themes and language? Why is it there?

Whole-text questions: open text

1 'Claudio's willingness to marry the "cousin" of Hero exposes the superficial nature of the society Shakespeare creates in this play.' Do you agree with this view? In your answer you should include reference to Act V scene 1, from 'Enter Leonato and Antonio, with the Sexton' (line 245) to the end of the scene.

Examiner's comments

- All candidates considered the scene suggested to them, but weaker ones failed to expand their argument by discussing Messinian society as a whole.
- More successful answers introduced further examples from the play, and some argued that it reflected Shakespeare's own society.
- The best candidates considered the play as a dramatic construct and commented on how form, structure and language shape the text's meaning.
- Important social patterns worth discussing included: patriarchy; social hierarchies in Messina; the role of the military in forming relationships.
- Sophisticated answers often judged Claudio in the light of the play's genre.
- Some strong candidates discussed differing notions of superficiality between periods in history, particularly in relation to different rituals of courtship.
- The Beatrice/Benedick relationship was usefully contrasted to the Claudio/Hero relationship.
- Weaker answers failed to engage with what 'superficial' meant, and focused too narrowly on the Claudio/Hero relationship without considering the society as a whole.

(Edexcel examiner's report, summer 2005)

Further questions

2 What do the scenes involving Dogberry and his watchmen contribute to the total dramatic effect of *Much Ado About Nothing*? In your answer you should consider the following:

- the relationship of these scenes to the play's plot and themes
- dialogue, and any effects of language
- actions, properties, costume and use of the performing space

3 'Claudio is an immature and foolish boy.' How far do you agree with this view?

4 What is the significance of music and dance in the play as a whole?

5 What is the effect of the time scheme utilised in the play?

6 How significant is Messina as a setting for the play's action?

7 To what extent do you think *Much Ado About Nothing* can be described accurately as a 'problem play'?

8 'Leonato is a caring father whose trust is tragically misplaced.' How far do you agree with this view?

9 Is there any evidence in the play to support the view that deception can sometimes be justified?

10 Examine Shakespeare's treatment of the themes of misunderstanding and disguise in *Much Ado About Nothing*.

11 Discuss Shakespeare's treatment of forgiveness and reconciliation in the play.

12 Explore the significance of the lack of mother figures in the play.

13 Explore the different uses and meanings of love in the play.

Passage-based essay questions

The question you choose may direct you to a prescribed passage or ask you to select your own. Either way you will need to show your knowledge of the whole play as well as your response to and analysis of a particular sequence. Careful selection of passages is crucial to ensure the relevance and success of the essay; the passages you like or are most familiar with are not necessarily the most appropriate for a particular title. Do not waste time paraphrasing what happens in the scene or the content of the speech or dialogue; just give a quick summary of its setting and context, along the lines of who is present and why, what has just happened, what will follow, and what its dramatic purpose is.

Examiners advise that reference to the rest of the work should be as much as 60% of the essay even for a passage-based question. Focus closely on the passage but also relate its content and/or language to other parts of the text, backwards and forwards, and link your comments to the overall themes and/or structure of the play. Include references to character, event, theme and language, and ask how the extract modifies or adds to our understanding so far, and how typical it is of the work as a whole. Think about audience reaction, using your own as the basis for your response.

Passage-based questions: prescribed

1 Look again at Act I scene 1 from Claudio: 'O, my lord' (275) to the end of the scene. Using a detailed examination of this sequence as a starting point, explore

the ways in which Shakespeare presents the men in *Much Ado About Nothing* as 'looking with a soldier's eye'. (*Edexcel, unit 3b, June 2001*)

Ideas for a plan

- Analyse the language used by Don Pedro and Claudio, and what this reveals about their attitude to love (e.g. the medical metaphor suggested by 'minister', 'salved', 'remedy').
- Consider the idea suggested by Claudio in his opening speech that war and love are incompatible.
- Contextualise the Elizabethan view of the lover and soldier.
- Look for examples where the men in the play behave like soldiers and/or lovers.
- Introduce the idea that men discussing women in their absence is a social norm in Messina.
- Suggest the advantages and disadvantages of this approach to a successful courtship and/or marriage.
- Consider Don Pedro's role in the wooing of Hero, and its consequences.
- Ensure that the other important men of the play are also discussed; for example, consider whether Leonato (who is not a soldier) treats Hero any better than the military men in the play.
- Discuss Benedick and Don Pedro's influence over Claudio.
- Analyse Benedick's conversion from misogynist to lover, considering whether or not he and his male companions change their perspectives over the course of the play.

Further questions

2 Remind yourself of Act V scene 1, from Benedick's entrance at line 110 to his exit at line 186. How does this passage help you understand the male characters and the way their relationships change over the course of the play?

3 BEATRICE: Stand I condemned for pride and scorn so much? (III.1.108)
Do you agree that Shakespeare presents the character of Beatrice as 'offending against society's expectations about women'? You should include in your answer an examination of Act III scene 1 and at least one other extract of your own choice.

4 Analyse the passage from Benedick's speech in Act I scene 1 beginning 'That a woman conceived me, I thank her' (220) to his exit at line 268. What is its dramatic effect, and how does it relate to the main themes of the play?

5 Remind yourself of Act I scene 3. What do you think this contributes to our understanding of Don John's character and motivation in the play?

6 'Men were deceivers ever'. In your view, is this how Shakespeare presents men in the world of the play? You should include in your answer reference to Act II scene 3 (from the beginning of the scene to *'Exit Balthasar'*, line 90.)

7 'In *Much Ado About Nothing*, Shakespeare dramatises the conflict between love and friendship.' Explore Shakespeare's presentation of love and friendship in the light of this comment. In your answer you should include an examination of Act IV scene 1 (from 'Lady Beatrice, have you wept all this while?', line 253, to the end of the scene).

8 Look again at Don John's deception of Claudio and Don Pedro in Act III scene 2, from Don John's entrance at line 72 to the end of the scene. Using this speech as a starting point, consider Claudio's relationship with his male companions in the play as a whole.

9 'The whole of *Much Ado About Nothing* depends on illusions and deceptions: they are the foundation of the world of the play.' In the light of this quotation, examine the ways in which Shakespeare explores 'illusions and deceptions' in *Much Ado About Nothing*. You should include in your answer an examination of Act I scenes 2 and 3.

10 Look again at Beatrice's conversation about marriage with Antonio and Leonato in Act II scene 1, beginning at line 16 and ending at line 76. What does this passage contribute to your understanding of the themes of marriage and obedience in the play?

11 'The masked ball is a microcosm of the play.' Look again at the Act II scene 1 and explain whether you agree or disagree with this view.

12 Look again at Leonato's speech in Act IV scene 1, beginning 'Wherefore! Why, doth not every earthly thing / Cry shame upon her?' (118) and ending at line 141. How does it illuminate Leonato's character, and his relationship with Hero?

13 Look again at Act I scene 1, from the opening exchange between Leonato and the Messenger to the arrival of Don Pedro's party in line 88. How does this passage establish the relationships between different characters, and how do they change as the play goes on?

14 Look again at Act V scene 4. To what extent do you find it a satisfactory conclusion to the play?

15 Look again at the gulling of Beatrice in Act III scene 1. How far do you consider it to be a comic scene? Explain whether or not you find it convincing and/or amusing.

Passage-based questions: selected

1 Select and analyse a sequence that explores the relationship between Leonato and Hero.

Ideas for plan

- Leonato's response to Hero's rejection in Act IV scene 1 is a key passage.
- Other useful scenes may feature Leonato making decisions in Hero's absence, or talking about her whilst she is silently present.
- Relevant themes include family, loyalty, honour, love.
- Leonato is in many ways a traditional father.
- Hero is generally a humble and obedient daughter.
- The play reflects the perspective of a patriarchal society.
- Leonato's willingness to believe the slander against his daughter in Act IV scene 1 shows the importance of female virginity, and the power of rumour.

- It could be argued that Leonato's choice of husband for Hero is socially advantageous for him, and he does not mind whom she marries as long as they are well connected.
- Hero's behaviour in Act III scene 1 and Act III scene 5 shows that she is confident and forthright in the company of other women.
- Leonato's assertion in Act V scene 1 'My soul doth tell me Hero is belied' (42) shows his guilt for turning on her in Act IV.
- Leonato's challenge to Claudio in Act V scene 1 shows him resuming the role of Hero's protector.
- Students should consider whether Hero and Leonato are fully reconciled at the end of the play.

2 **'It is the warmth and apparent equality of the relationship between Beatrice and Benedick that appeals to the audience today.' Do you agree with this response to Shakespeare's presentation of the relationship between Beatrice and Benedick? You should include in your answer an examination of at least two appropriate extracts.**

Examiner's comments

- Some essays spent too long on the early scenes between Beatrice and Benedick, failing to deal with the key phrases 'apparent equality' and 'the audience today' in sufficient detail.
- Some students tended to deal with Beatrice's appeal to modern audiences rather than considering modern interpretations of her relationship with Benedick.
- The relationship between Claudio and Hero provides a useful contrast, but the emphasis of the essay should be on Beatrice and Benedick.
- Some excellent essays linked the idea of 'apparent equality' to the genre of comedy.
- The best essays considered Beatrice and Benedick as dramatic constructs and discussed the warmth with which Shakespeare presents his creations.
- More successful answers showed a sophisticated understanding of the balance between Beatrice and Benedick, and considered how contextual factors affected the way the couple are, or have been, perceived.
- Very good answers picked up on the phrase 'apparent equality', discussing how the equality can actually be considered to be merely superficial.
- Close analysis of the text was crucial for those candidates who successfully discussed the paradoxes in both characters' behaviour.

(Edexcel examiner's report, summer 2005)

Further questions

3 **A recent critical opinion about *Much Ado About Nothing* is that Beatrice and Benedick are 'tricked into marriage against their hearts: without social pressure they would have remained unmarried'. Do you agree that this is how Shakespeare presents their relationship? You should refer to at least two sequences.**

4 'Don John is an anti-social outsider in the play, since he is effectively excluded from the family network.' Is this how you interpret Shakespeare's presentation of the character of Don John? In your answer you should refer to at least two extracts.

5 Select and analyse two passages that illuminate Claudio's relationship with Hero.

6 'In *Much Ado About Nothing* Shakespeare presents a society heavily dependent on, and sometimes misled by, the ways in which people perceive one another.' How do you respond to this view of the play? You should include in your answer an examination of at least two appropriate extracts.

7 'What must particularly strike a modern audience is the extent to which a young woman's conduct is influenced by the presence of a father.' In the light of this statement, what is your response to Shakespeare's dramatic presentation of Hero and Beatrice in *Much Ado About Nothing*? In your answer you should include reference to at least two extracts from the play.

8 Select two passages as a starting point and explain the dramatic significance of the Dogberry/Watch/Conrade/Borachio subplot.

9 Anna Brownell Jameson once claimed that 'In Beatrice, high intellect and high animal spirits meet, and excite each other like fire and air.' Select two scenes from the play that help you explore this view.

10 Charles Gildon wrote that 'this play we must call a comedy, tho' some of the incidents and discourses are more in a tragic strain'. Select two passages which explore the importance of tragedy in the play.

11 Select two scenes that show contrasting aspects of Benedick's character and explain which of these seem to you most characteristic of him.

12 DOGBERRY: This is the end of the charge: you, constable, are to present the Prince's own person; if you meet the Prince in the night, you may stay him.

VERGES: Nay, by'r Lady, that I think 'a cannot.

DOGBERRY: Five shillings to one on't, with any man that knows the statutes, he may stay him.

In the light of this exchange consider the view that in *Much Ado About Nothing* Shakespeare 'deliberately turns the expected social order on its head'. You should base your answer on a detailed examination of at least two appropriate sequences of your choice.

Sample essays

Below are two sample essays of different types written by different students. Both of them have been assessed as falling within the top band. You can judge them against the Assessment Objectives for this text for your exam board and decide on the mark you think each deserves and why. You will also be able to see ways in which each could be improved in terms of content, style and accuracy.

Sample essay 1

BEATRICE: **Stand I condemned for pride and scorn so much?** (Act III scene 1)
**Do you agree that Shakespeare presents the character of Beatrice as 'offending
against society's expectations about women'? You should include in your answer
an examination of Act III scene 1 and at least one other extract of your own choice.**

Beatrice and all the other characters around her are products of the society Shakespeare
puts them in. *Much Ado About Nothing* is set in Italy, but Messina still represents many
of the opinions that would have been current in the England of his day. Despite the fact
that Queen Elizabeth I was on the throne, these ideas included the view that women were
naturally inferior to men, that fathers should decide who their daughters married and that
women had almost no concept of independence at all.

Beatrice challenges all of these expectations in Act II scene 1, the ball scene. Within
twenty lines of the start of the scene, Leonato tells his niece that 'thou wilt never get thee
a husband if thou be so shrewd of thy tongue'. By saying this, Leonato shows us that
marriage is the conventional goal of any young woman, and that Beatrice's outspoken
behaviour means that she will not be able to fulfil the social expectation that she will marry,
as women were supposed to be quiet and obedient in the presence of men.

Beatrice's opposition to the established social convention of marriage provides a
clear contrast with the views of her cousin, Hero. Hero is far more representative of the
women of her time. When her uncle Antonio asks if she will be 'ruled by your father' in the
matter of choosing a husband, Hero does not even answer. Instead, Beatrice highlights
her cousin's obedience by replying in her place 'Yes, faith; it is my cousin's duty to make
curtsy and say, "Father as it please you"'. Beatrice's ability to make such acute social observations means that the men around her find it very difficult to assert their patriarchal ideals.
Even Benedick can find no answer to some of Beatrice's railing, declaring 'I cannot endure
my Lady Tongue' and then leaving the scene before she can harass him further.

The difference in Leonato's treatment of the two young women under his guardian-
ship also shows that he is far less confident handling Beatrice than his own daughter.
When Beatrice draws attention to Don Pedro's inability to find a wife by jokingly refusing
his proposal, Leonato is unable to tell her off for embarrassing his grand guest, and
instead makes up an excuse to get rid of her: 'Niece, will you look to those things I told
you of?'

Act II scene 1 therefore shows Beatrice at her most subversive, defying the expectations of her society and standing up for herself. However, we see a quite different part
of her personality in Act III scene 1. In this gulling scene, we see a softer, more vulnerable
side to her.

After she overhears the criticism Hero makes of her that 'Nature never framed a
woman's heart / Of prouder stuff than that of Beatrice', she is quick to see the truth in some
of her cousin's words. She is silent as Hero and Ursula say that her 'swift and excellent'
wit is often used to turn 'every man the wrong side out'. From the evidence of the play's

early scenes, Hero's language contains an element of truth, and Beatrice is remarkably quick to change her attitude.

At the end of the scene she asks herself 'Stand I condemned for pride and scorn so much?' and even looks forward to Benedick's love 'taming my wild heart'. This suggests that much of her subversive behaviour is a front designed to protect her from being hurt in the game of love, a game which women had very little control over. In many ways, she wishes (like another of Shakespeare's famous shrews, Katharina in *The Taming of the Shrew*) to be a part of the society she derides, but she wishes to do so without giving up her dignity.

This interpretation of Beatrice's attitude is crucial to our view of whether or not she offends against society's expectations. Although she certainly does not fulfil the female stereotype of the period, Beatrice is not what you might call an 'offensive' character. If she is offensive, her offence is amusing, and highlights the weakness and hypocrisy at the heart of Messina's patriarchal society in a light-hearted way. This is certainly true today even more than it was in Shakespeare's time. If Beatrice can be seen as 'offending against society's expectations', it is only fair to point out that Elizabethan society's expectations about women now seem archaic. Although audiences have always enjoyed her character's wit, a modern audience has the benefit of doing so without seeing a strong woman as a novelty. Far from being a 'harpy' to a twenty-first century audience, Beatrice is the heart and soul of the play.

I can only agree that, in terms of her forthright and uncompromising attitude, Beatrice is offensive to the expectations of sixteenth-century society. On the other hand, this is where her charm and depth of personality lies. Shakespeare is also careful to avoid presenting her as too subversive a force. By enabling Beatrice to find a witty and amusing match in Benedick, Shakespeare ensures that she does not exist entirely outside the established order of the play.

Sample essay 2

What do the scenes involving Dogberry and his Watchmen contribute to the total dramatic effect of *Much Ado About Nothing*? In your answer you should consider the following:

- **the relationship of these scenes to the play's plot and themes**
- **dialogue, and any effects of language**
- **actions, properties, costume and use of the performing space**

Dogberry and his watchmen spend far less time on stage than almost every other character in *Much Ado About Nothing*, and their scenes are usually the first to be cut by directors who are anxious about the length of the play. Nonetheless, their dramatic function in the play is much more important than it may initially appear, and they contribute a lot to the total dramatic effect of the play, in a number of different ways.

Apart from anything else, the plot of the play would be totally different if Dogberry and his companions were absent. Although they are inept, the truth of Borachio and Don John's plan is only discovered because the watchmen overhear Borachio boasting about it, and Dogberry extracts a confession from the two men. In addition to their important plot function, these scenes tell us a great deal about many of the play's central themes. With their misuse of language and inept policing, Dogberry and his men represent Messina's lower classes. When Leonato comes to see Dogberry before Hero and Claudio's planned wedding, he speaks brutally and unpleasantly, saying 'Neighbours, you are tedious'. This is in stark contrast to Leonato's colourful and flattering language to important dignitaries like Don Pedro. Class is certainly an issue for Dogberry, who tries very hard to show his importance in society by using long and complicated words. He believes that 'to read and write comes by nature', and therefore suggests that people who are literate (as he thinks he is) are innately superior to those who aren't. Unfortunately, Dogberry's language is more ambitious than successful, as he uses or pronounces words incorrectly time and again. He tells Leonato that he and his men have 'comprehended two aspicious persons' (instead of 'apprehended' two 'suspicious' people) and asks his scribe to 'set down our excommunication', once again showing that his grasp of words is loose. In a class system like Messina's, themes of service, loyalty and pride are also very important. Dogberry's respect for the upper classes shows that he is loyal in trying to serve them, but also raises the question of whether he is most concerned about doing so in order to elevate himself in society. In contrast, Leonato's disdain for the police force contributes to his own misery; he is punished for his arrogance and pride by going through the agony of seeing Hero publicly disgraced when it could have been avoided.

However you look at it, all of Dogberry's incompetence adds an important extra dimension to the dramatic force of the performance: humour. In Shakespeare's day, theatre was a much more inclusive form of entertainment, and rich audience members would sit while poorer people stood in the 'pit' at the front of the stage. The Dogberry subplot would appeal to a wide audience because more educated people could laugh at his unintentional use of malapropisms, while less sophisticated viewers could still enjoy the slapstick elements of the arrests and questioning scenes. Both audiences would also have appreciated that the bumbling police officer and his men increase the tension as we wonder whether Don John's evil plot will be foiled in time. Some directors have even chosen to show the interrogation of Conrade and Borachio going on silently on one half of the stage whilst Claudio disgraces Hero at the church on the other, building the tension even further.

As I have discussed, Dogberry and his men provide an important element of humour to a performance of the play. However, a lot of the amusing malapropisms Dogberry uses would not be understood by a twenty-first century audience. Because of this, his lines and his watchmen's lines are often cut to shorten the play. When this happens, these characters can still be a source of almost slapstick comedy, particularly if they are cast well and put in the right costume. Most actors play Dogberry as an overweight and pompous character, whose very presence on the stage is able to draw a laugh. Others put him in a gaudy and over-the-top uniform to emphasise how ridiculous he is. If his watchmen are dressed in matching colours, to show that they are under his command, this can also emphasise the part of Dogberry's character that desires social mobility and power.

Overall, the scenes featuring Dogberry and his watchmen contribute a great deal to the dramatic function of *Much Ado About Nothing*. Although they are not at the centre of it, they control parts of the plot and show a totally different side of Messinian society than we would otherwise see. They also provide an important comic outlet for a play which is, after all, a comedy. This changes the whole tone of the play and provides light-hearted amusement, which contrasts with the more serious scenes in the play. Although the time they spend on stage is relatively short, *Much Ado About Nothing* is a much richer play for the dramatic input of Dogberry and his men.

Further study

Books

Brown, J.R. (ed.) (1979) *'Much Ado About Nothing' and 'As You Like It': A Casebook*, Macmillan.

Bullough, Geoffrey (ed.) (1975) *Narrrative and Dramatic Sources of Shakespeare*, vol. 2, Routledge.

Cookson, L. and Loughrey, B. (1989) *Critical Essays on 'Much Ado About Nothing'*, Longman.

Friedman, M.D. (2002) *The World Must Be Peopled: Shakespeare's Comedies of Forgiveness*, chapter 3, London and Toronto: Associated University Presses.

Gay, P. (1994) As *She Likes It: Shakespeare's Unruly Women*, Routledge.

Leggatt, A. (1974) *Shakespeare's Comedy of Love*, chapter 7, Methuen.

Levin, R.A. (1985) *Love and Society in Shakespearean Comedy*, chapter 4, London and Toronto: Associated University Presses.

Sales, R. (1989) *'Much Ado About Nothing': A Critical Study*, Penguin.

Tillyard, E.M.W. (1943) *The Elizabethan World Picture*, Chatto and Windus.

Tillyard, E.M.W. (1965) *Shakespeare's Early Comedies*, Chatto and Windus.

Films

Much Ado About Nothing has inspired several film versions, most of which adhere fairly closely to Shakespeare's text. Some of the more memorable ones include:

1967: Alan Cooke's film developed out of Franco Zeffirelli's stage version, and was recorded for television. Starring Maggie Smith and Robert Stephens, with Derek Jacobi as Don Pedro, it was well received by critics before Zeffirelli went on to direct *Romeo and Juliet* on film in 1969.

1973: like Cooke and Zeffirelli's 1967 production, director A. J. Antoon's film grew out of a successful stage run. However, the success of his onscreen American 'rag-time' version caused box-office sales for the stage production to fall, prematurely ending its run.

1984: the BBC version, directed by Stuart Burge, is a fairly unspectacular production, which takes few risks with the play and likewise offers little fresh insight into it. It stars Cherie Lunghi and Robert Lindsay.

1993: Kenneth Branagh's all-star production features Emma Thompson, Richard Briers, Keanu Reeves, Michael Keaton, Imelda Staunton and Kate Beckinsale. It was shot in Tuscany's rolling countryside, evoking the feel of Shakespeare's pastoral 'green' comedies. This version of the play is amusing, light-hearted and probably its most famous incarnation to date.

2005: writer David Nicholl's modern BBC adaptation (Dir. Brian Percival) is witty and innovative, though Shakespeare's text is virtually absent. Beatrice is cast as a television presenter who is forced to work with old rival Benedick on her evening news show, whilst Don (Don John) is portrayed as an obsessive former lover of Hero's, who is motivated by jealousy. It is worth watching just for Hero's spirited rejection of Claude (Claudio) at the end of the film. See the website link below for more details.

Internet

There is now a vast number of sites on the internet with material on Shakespeare and *Much Ado About Nothing*. Google is a useful search engine, particularly if you can modify your search with key words like 'eavesdropping', 'honour', 'music', or the names of key characters. Remember, however, that although the standard of internet resources is improving all the time, the quality of information available is highly variable. Websites are set up and closed down with bewildering rapidity, and material is not always accurate. Some websites also charge for access to their resources, and it is difficult to judge whether or not they provide good value before parting with money. Similar material can often be found for free if you are patient and thorough in your use of search engines.

- **www.shakespeare.palomar.edu/** (*Mr William Shakespeare and the Internet*) is one of the best general Shakespeare sites. It includes general information and an extensive set of links to other sites, many of which include the full text of some or all of the plays. Most of these have some form of search engine, which allows the text to be searched for words and phrases, as at **www.online-literature.com/shakespeare/muchado/**

As far as *Much Ado About Nothing* is concerned, there are a number of sites, and subsections of more general Shakespeare sites, One example is:

- **www.sparknotes.com/shakespeare/muchado/** is a good introductory site, with the full text, notes and search engine.

For a more lighthearted take on the play, see:

- **www.bbc.co.uk/drama/shakespeare/muchadoaboutnothing/** — an amusing and engaging multimedia site that looks at the recent BBC adaptation of the play, and includes interviews and clips from the production. This is particularly helpful for students grappling with the difficulties of interpreting a play that is over 400 years old.

Images from various productions of *Much Ado About Nothing* can be found by entering the names of particular characters into Google's image search, along with the word 'Shakespeare'. Artists' impressions of the play and its characters, as well as postcards of productions and characters through the ages, are available by following the excellent links at:

- **http://shakespeare.emory.edu/**

Other useful websites:

- **www.shakespeares-globe.org/** is the official website of the reconstructed Globe Theatre.
- **www.bl.uk/treasures/shakespeare/homepage.html** offers a quarto view of Shakespeare's works.
- **www.shakespeare.org.uk** is the site of the Shakespeare Birthplace Trust.